PENDELL HOUSE

This book is dedicated to our lovely daughter, Amanda, who tragically succumbed to cancer in October 2015. She was the driving force behind the many improvements to Pendell House and its garden, which she loved, during her and her husband David's ownership 1997–2005.

PENDELL HOUSE

Blechingley
1636–2016

JIM BROWN

JIM BROWN is a former detective with the Southampton City Police and Chief Security & Safety Officer on the Southampton Container Terminal. He lived and worked in the city for 82 years before moving to Caterham in 2014, with his wife, to be with their family. In retirement he became a well-known Southampton local historian and author and Vice President of Bitterne Local History Society.

He has written and contributed to a number of books and booklets on the history of Southampton, including *The Illustrated History of Southampton's Suburbs; Southampton's Changing Faces; More Southampton Changing Faces; Southampton Murder Victims Volumes One and Two; Southampton's Lucky Jim; Southampton's Lost Pubs; Townhill Park House; The Sad Tale of Richard Parker; Building the Itchen Bridge; Henry Brain, A Victorian & Edwardian Photographer; The Story of St Andrews Methodist Church, Sholing; The Story of the Southampton Salvation Army Sholing Corps, 1897–2008;* and *Bridging the Itchen.* Many are available on Amazon and as ebooks.

He and his wife now live on the site of the former Guards Depot and Barracks, and his first booklet on moving there was *Caterham – From Barracks to Village*, an account of how the estate was created after the Brigade of Guards finally left in 1995. This was followed by *The Story of the Croydon Citadel Corps No. 9 1869–2016*, a well-illustrated history of the 4th oldest active Salvation Army Corps in the world, containing a large number of photos published for the first time.

First Published in Great Britain in 2017 by DB Publishing,
an imprint of JMD Media Ltd

© Jim Brown, 2017

ISBN 978-1-78091-552-4

Printed and bound in the UK

CONTENTS

ACKNOWLEDGEMENTS

John HESKETH and Alan JOHNSON for passing on their initial research into the history of Pendell House and John for supplying further information; the late Peter Jack GRAY (1933–2001) for his booklet *Blechingley Village & Parish*; Peter HEATHER of the East Surrey Family History Society for researching material for me at their Advice & Research Centre in Lingfield; Dame Sarah GOAD for allowing me to quote extensively from her grandfather's 1921 book *Blechingley: A Parish History* and her father's 1949 book *Blechingley*; Tom FRY, Tandridge Planning Department, for supplying copies of planning applications for Pendell House; Kate DURRANT of Historic England for supplying the Grade I listing details for Pendell House; Charles STURGE for supplying detailed information about his family; Sue DOWN for letting me use her drawing of the Glyd coat of arms and for supplying much GLYD family history; Amanda MOTT for supplying her ancestor's photos and a good deal of family material supplied by her father, Michael MOTT; Eleanor YATES, Hampshire Industrial Archaeological Society for allowing their photos of ice houses to be used; Alice HOWARD, Picture Library Assistant, Ashmolean Museum of Art and Archaeology, University of Oxford for supplying and allowing reproduction of their Gainsborough painting, my editor, Dan COXON, for transforming my text and photos into this book and finally Matthew LIMBERT for the design.

All unattributed pictures were either taken by the author or were in the possession of his late daughter.

Special thanks go to Derek MOORE, Chairman of the Blechingley Conservation & Historical Society, for allowing me to copy a number of his personal papers and photos and Richard FOWLER, Secretary, for scanning extracts from a number of Bletchingley books held by the Society and both for proofreading a draft version of this book. Richard also loaned me his precious copy of Lambert's 1921 *Blechingley – A Parish History*, which proved invaluable in obtaining details of various families. Their combined generous and willing help was priceless.

BIBLIOGRAPHY

Blechingley – A Parish History (1921) by Uvedale LAMBERT

Blechingley (1949) by Uvedale H. H. LAMBERT Jnr

Blechingley Village & Parish (1991) by Peter Jack GRAY

Article in *Blechingley Magazine*, October 1996 by Derek MOORE

Victoria County History, Surrey, volume IV (1912) by H. E. MAIDEN

The Buildings of England; Surrey (1971) by N. PEVSNER

Ice & Icehouses Through the Ages (1982) by Monica ELLIS

Portrait of a Family (1987) by Eric Alston MOTT

St Mary the Virgin, Bletchingley, Surrey (2005) by the Parish Church

1. INTRODUCTION

Courtesy of Hamptons International

This estate agent's modern advert shows the 17th-century Pendell House in Pendell Road, Bletchingley, Surrey. It was purchased in 1997 by my son-in-law David, then 43, and daughter Amanda Milner-Brown, 42, who lived there with their three young sons until 2005.

It was described as:

> *A magnificent Grade 1 listed 17th Century country residence, with superb family accommodation arranged over four floors. Supported by grounds extending to approximately 13 acres and incorporating a 1.7 acre walled garden, heated swimming pool and tennis court.*

The accommodation was described as:

Magnificent Reception Hall, Drawing Room, Sitting Room, Dining Room, Kitchen, Magnificent Guest Cloakroom, WC, Cellar Area (containing a Wine Store, Workroom, Two Further Storage Areas, Sauna and an Original Prayer Room), Study, Master Bedroom with En Suite Bathroom, Seven Further Bedrooms, Three with En Suite Facilities.

Pendell House received its Grade 1 listing on 11 June 1958. The property was then described as:

House. dated 1636. Red brick in English bond, deep eaves to plain tiled hipped roof; end stacks with cut brick panels and decoration on shafts. Symmetrical plan about narrow central hall with staircase to the rear. two storeys over cellar with attics under two flat roof sash window dormers, plat band over ground floor. Five bays, centre bay projecting and rising to three floors with pediment above and rusticated ground floor. Glazing bar sash windows in moulded surrounds through-out, ground floor windows under segmental brick arches, alternating with cut brick recessed panels in the form of pilasters in reverse complete with recessed capitals. Central doubled arched half glazed doors in stone surround. Right hand return front: two glazing bar sash windows to first floor, diamond and circle patterning to chimney stacks.

Left hand return front (garden front): four bays over rendered basement. three flat roofed dormers above. Plaque on chimney reads 'RGE 1636'. Rear wing to left with steep pediment over arched glazing bar casement window. Arched door to left of centre under stone plat band moulding continued at lower level over the remainder of the ground floor.

Interior: little of the original features remain. Cornice and acanthus frieze to ground floor room to left. Marble fireplace surround with fan decoration and drapery swags. Baroque style fireplace surround to ground floor room front left with gadroon type moulding and scroll bracket decoration. Square return staircase to rear of hall with foliage and scroll iron balustrade.

Inigo JONES.

It is one of only a handful of houses attributed to England's first classical architect, Inigo JONES, (1573–1652), that is still inhabited as a private house. Until Inigo JONES, 'Tudor' was the dominant style for even the grandest of houses, as the classical architectural ideas following the Renaissance had not reached England.

The *Country Life* magazine of 14 March 1968 stated Pendell House was for sale for £32,500 and had three reception rooms, nine bedrooms, four bathrooms, with oil-fired central heating and stood in 21 acres of grounds, with two cottages.

It added that in his authoritative book on Inigo JONES, Sir John Summerson said: 'the figure of Jones is obscured by such a swarm of misattributions that the toil of discernment enfeebles perception.' The book went on to say that:

> *Amazingly, there are only seven surviving buildings whose records are authenticated as being by Jones. One of the most puzzling of the houses traditionally associated with his name is Pendell House, which has a rigidly symmetrically layout typical of Jones. The stone staircase is similar to, and contemporary with, the staircase at the Queen's House in Greenwich, which Jones undoubtedly designed. Professor Nikolaus Pevsner suggests that Inigo Jones may have supplied the plan and some general guidance, but left the elevations to be worked up by the mason.*

Inigo was the son of a Welsh cloth worker, his Christian name was the same as his father and is believed to be a Spanish version of Ignatius. In 1610, he was appointed Surveyor to Henry Frederick, Prince of Wales. In September 1615, he was promoted to Surveyor General of the King's Works, marking the beginning of his career in earnest. In 1616, he began work on the Queen's House, Greenwich, for James I's wife, Anne of Denmark. Work stopped when she died in 1619 but was resumed in 1629, this time for James I's Queen Henrietta Maria. It was finished in 1635 as the first strictly classical building in England, employing ideas found in the architecture of Palladio and ancient Rome. It is JONES' earliest surviving work. It is noteworthy that the smaller staircase in the Queen's House, one of the earliest examples of an 'open' staircase with no central support, is similar to that in Pendell House, lending credence to the suggestion that Inigo JONES was involved.

Investigations also suggest that Pendell House always had the two sash windows in the east side of the house. If so, it may be the very first example in England of a house with such fenestration. It is also worthy of note that Inigo JONES is alleged to have introduced such windows into England, probably from Holland. The term is used almost exclusively to refer to windows where the glazed panels are opened by sliding vertically, or horizontally, in a style known as a 'Yorkshire light', sliding sash, or sash and case (so called because the weights are concealed in a box case).

The oldest known surviving examples of sash windows installed in England were in the 1670s at Ham House, near Richmond. Originally built in 1610, it was transformed in 1672 by the Duke of Lauderdale, a key member of King Charles' inner cabinet, when it is believed the sash windows were installed.

The author was delighted to find that he was able to discover a good deal of information about the various families who have lived in Pendell House over the centuries, with varying degrees of success. Many ancestors and/or descendants were found to be individuals of some distinction, and a number of incidents involving the house are of great interest to anybody having personal knowledge of the building.

2. BRIEF HISTORY OF BLECHINGLEY & PENDELL MANOR

One must first give a brief mention of the history of Blechingley, a parish that stretches from the crest of the Downs in the north to Outwood Common in the south; from Godstone Green in the east to the M23 in the west. It includes the ancient hamlets of Brewer Street, Chevington, as well as Pendell, with medieval hunting taking place in North Park and South Park.

It should be noted that the 't', now commonly used in Bletchingley, appeared in the late 18th century and was used by strangers, not locals. It became more frequently used by London lawyers and as Deeds increased in number, so did the inserted 't' become more common. When the Post Officer then used it, this spelling of the ancient Borough was changed for all time, even though, according to Uvedale Lambert, it was 'etymologically untrue and historically inaccurate'.

Although man obviously roamed the area for thousands of years, there is little firm evidence of his presence until the Iron Age, when a camp was built at the top of White Hill. It was a Mesolithic site. A Roman villa found near Pendell over 100 years ago proves that the Romans knew the area and farmed parts of the fertile Vale of Holmesdale. Nothing now remains of the villa but there is little doubt that it was the centre of an estate, one of several along the foot of the Downs in both Surrey and Kent. Modern aerial photographs have shown evidence of a larger building nearby that has yet to be excavated.

The main evidence for Saxon occupation of the area comes from the name Blechingley. Its *'inga'* element suggests a 7th or 8th century origin and it probably means the *'leah'* or clearing of the sons *'ing'* of Blaeca. It may also derive from *'blaecan'*, the Anglo-Saxon to bleach, and *'ley'*, a clearing. It could therefore mean a clearing where bleaching fabric took place. There is a link, before the Domesday Book, of local fuller's earth deposits and the woollen trade.

Blechingley's origins lie in a Norman estate which stretches beyond Outwood to the modern county boundary in the south. The Domesday Book, with later documents and marks on the landscape, means one can begin to decipher the extent of the Saxon estates. These, in due course, with many alterations, formed the modern parish.

The manors which were to become the modern parish referred to in the Domesday Book are:

> *Blachingelie is held Richard of Tonbridge of the King. Alfheah, Alwin and Alnoth held it from King Edward (the Confessor) ... There were three manors, now it is one ... Then it answered for 10 hides ... Richard holds Chevington. Alnoth held it from King Edward. Then it answered for 20 hides ... A mill ...*

Chevington (Chivington) was clearly much the largest of the manors and stretched from the Downs to the modern Surrey/Sussex border. The Saxon manors which amalgamated to go under the single name of Blechingley included Pendell. Some boundaries are marked even today by noticeable banks and ditches.

Few buildings, apart from the churches, are likely to be earlier than about 1400 and outside Blechingley village there are almost none older than about 1600. This is because of the former two large hunting parks which prevented building.

The first mention of Blechingley as a borough is in 1225, but it was not a lasting success. Comparison of the tolls between 1296 and 1325 suggest that the market started to fail in the early 14th century. A combination of competition from the market at Reigate and the Black Death is a possible cause.

Queen Anne of Cleves, the unhappy and ill-favoured fourth wife of Henry VIII, was given Blechingley and a generous pension in 1540, when her marriage to Henry was annulled after only seven months. Blechingley then passed to Sir Thomas Cawarden, a keen Reformer, in 1547, when Anne became the owner of Richmond Palace and Hever Castle. After Elizabeth came to the throne he fell out of favour and died in the Tower in 1559. He is buried on the right-hand side of Blechingley Church high altar.

The evidence of the buildings suggests that there was a distinct revival in fortunes in the later 15th and early 16th century, but that thereafter the town stagnated so that there was little development until at least the 19th century. As a consequence, the village retains many of the medieval features that make it so attractive.

The historic northern boundary of Blechingley is 100 metres or so north of the M25 motorway. As it meanders along hedgerows it suggests it was set out when the parish was demarcated, probably sometime before 1300. The modern parish boundary is on top of the Downs and dates from the reorganisation of local government in 1894.

Pendell is almost certainly the second of the three Saxon manors which were amalgamated to form the Norman manor of Blechingley. Its extent in the late Saxon period was no more than the land between the Downs and the greensand ridge. The Roman remains were roughly in the centre of this estate, which may not be a coincidence.

The name, shown as 'Pendhill' in 1451 and 'Pendchyll' in 1522, appears to be of Saxon origin, 'Pen' being an enclosure in some of the richest land of an early settlement and the earlier 'hill' descriptive of its location. The modern 'dell' is also obvious from its position.

The bounds of the manor were, on the east, the old trackway of Whitehill Lane, and on the west, another trackway which today is not so obvious. Roughly it is the continuation south of Hill Top Lane in Chaldon and is now largely obliterated by the motorway. The most significant part of the track still remains. It is the part where it goes over the old dam by Mill Cottage.

In c.1360 Pendell Manor was sold by John MAYU to Sir Thomas UVEDALE, who sold it c.1517 to Henry SAUNDER of Charlewood. It was later bought by George HOLMAN, a grocer of London, whose family had lived for many years in nearby Godstone. He built Pendell Court in 1624 and his son, a Cromwellian, sat in the 1654 Parliament. It then passed by inheritance to the SEYLIARDS, then SCULLARDS and then to the PERKINS family, who united it with Blechingley Manor.

In 1878 the Manor was bought by Sir George MACLAY, explorer and one-time Speaker of the New South Wales Parliament, and sold to William Abraham BELL in 1893. His son, William Archibald Juxon BELL, bequeathed the Lordship to Uvedale LAMBERT in his Will. It passed from him to his son-in-law, Timothy GOAD, the current Lord of the Manor, whose wife, Dame Sarah GOAD, is a former Lord Lieutenant of Surrey.

Pendell is noted for its fine houses nestling in the vale below Cockley Plantation. If there was ever a village here it would most probably have been located at the bottom of the hill near those houses. Any trace of such a village disappeared in the early 17th century when the present houses were built.

15

SUPPOSITITIOUS COAT ARMOUR FOR BLECHINGLEY, USED ON "HERALDIC CHINA."

1 and 4, Stafford; 2, d'Audley; 3, de Clare.

Representing a lordship of 16 generations.

(Courtesy of Dame Sarah GOAD)

(Much of the previous information was obtained from research carried out by Peter Jack GRAY, (1933–2001), Local Historian and Author, and published in his book *Blechingley Village & Parish* (1991).)

3. DESIGN AND CONSTRUCTION OF PENDELL HOUSE

Pendell House is a listed Grade 1 building 'of exceptional architectural and historic interest', a fact that creates financial and time-consuming problems for any owner wishing to alter any feature in the building, no matter how trivial. However, as this account will show, such a listing is more than justified in the case of Pendell House.

Prior to its construction, commenced in 1633 and completed by 1636, for Richard GLYD, a wealthy tallow chandler of London, there appears to have been a house on the site known as 'Schriches', so called since it was held by a John SCHRICHES in 1451. The fact that the cellar rooms to the south-east extend beyond the main walls of the house adds credence to this argument, and the arches in the basement do appear to be of an older design than the rest of the house.

THE BASEMENT

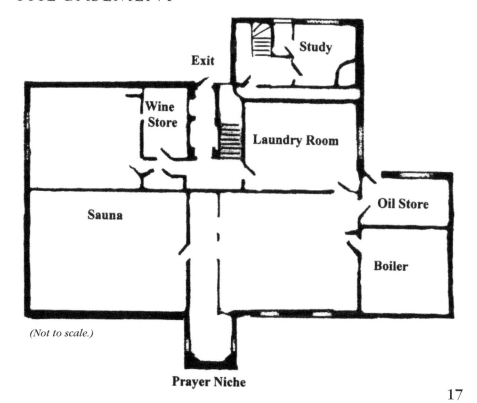

(Not to scale.)

Prayer Niche

A barrel-vaulted ceiling and distinctive storeroom door arches in the basement.

The arches in the entrance hall are distinctly different from those in the storeroom door arches.

(Courtesy of current owner of Pendell House.)

A further odd object in the basement is a well, within the building rather than constructed outside. It is a most unusual feature and indicates the age of the basement, possibly as early as the 1500s.

The main corridor in the basement runs from underneath the foot of the entry stairs to a small square space beneath the porch. This has been fitted out as a prayer niche complete with vaulting, arching and seating. The religion of Richard GLYD, the builder of Pendell House, is unknown, but the early 1600s were times of religious intolerance.

The Catholic Guy FAWKES had tried to blow up the Houses of Parliament in 1605, and when Pendell House was built King Charles I's extravagant form of worship, combined with the fact that his wife was Catholic, led many to suspect

that Charles was a secret Catholic. This strengthened the rapidly increasing religious movement known as Puritanism. The Puritan opposition to the King's actions increased their support, and this played an important role in favour of Parliament during the approaching Civil War. This hostility saw a growing movement to suppress Catholicism and other signs of the Roman Catholic faith. Richard GLYD may therefore have been a Catholic who wanted to keep his worship private as far as possible. This is only supposition, but it makes sense.

The culverts at front left and right of the entrance, the left-hand west one having what was said to be a small ice-house in the corner. It is suggested that this is the equivalent of the cook's refrigerator, with ice being replenished from a very large ice-house in the garden (the tunnel? – see later in 'The Garden & Grounds').

All rooms in the basement have superbly constructed barrel-vaulted ceilings. An almost unique feature of the basement is a substantial brick built culvert immediately beyond the foundation walls which almost surrounds the house.

Part of the spacious basement.

It provides air around the structure, thereby ensuring a much lower level of damp than might otherwise be expected. It is also an asset that the building is constructed on a rising that starts approximately 200 yards to the south.

A modern sauna (note the ceiling rings for hanging carcasses).

Basement room in the north-west quadrant, with more ceiling rings.

Basement entrance from under the main staircase.

Basement corridor leading to a north elevation lower exit.

Basement small store room.

North elevation lower exit, with coal and wood storage bunkers on left.

Note the two servant girls looking out of the top centre window.

The principal front elevation faces south, with the second main elevation facing west. The house therefore enjoys the best of light, particularly as it is raised and constructed on a rising that commences about 200 yards to the south.

Pendell House is a nearly square brick house of three storeys plus a basement. The original roofing was hipped with an inner valley and guttering where the inner slopes (not visible from the outside) joined and drained out through a concealed gutter, probably to the east. Later, very sensibly, the apexes were linked with a near flat section, enabling the whole underside of the roof to be accessible and ending the inner draining problem.

It is noteworthy that no screws, nails or bolts were used in the construction of the roof, merely wood dowels fixing the joints. The original lathes are still present in many areas.

The original kitchen, later used as a laundry area, is in the north-east quadrant of the basement, where there is a deep fireplace opening in the north walls. At a higher level are bread ovens feeding off the fireplace. Shortly after World War Two the STURGE family created the present kitchen on the first floor, changing the basement kitchen to a laundry area.

THE GROUND FLOOR

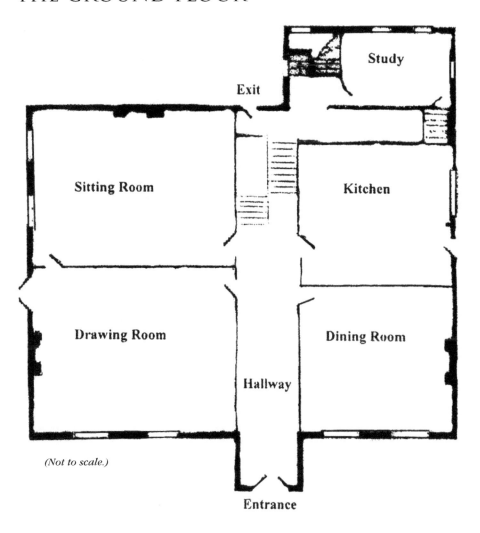

Study

Exit

Sitting Room

Kitchen

Drawing Room

Dining Room

Hallway

(Not to scale.)

Entrance

During the occupancy of the STURGE family (1936–1969) the Drawing Room was known as The Library and the Sitting Room was the Dining Room. The original Dining Room later became a Study.

In the main south elevation there is a three-storey porch built almost, but not precisely, at the centre of the façade. It has been alleged that it was built 60 years after the initial construction, but this cannot be proved. It is difficult to imagine why such an addition should be made at a later stage, there is little space gained and the expense would hardly have been justified.

It was far more likely part of the house when built in 1636 by Richard GLYD, whose initials appear carved in brick over the entrance. 'RG' can be clearly seen

The south front main elevation.

on the left side of the doorway, at the top of the lamp, but only the letter 'G' and the faint outline of a possible 'E' on the right side. If an 'E' (for Elizabeth, Richard's wife) it would strengthen the argument that the frontage was made in 1636.

The current owner of Pendell House kindly and very helpfully took this high-resolution photo of the right-hand initials. Taken at an angle. they show the letter 'G' very clearly, together with an upright mark that could either form part of the letter 'E' or possibly 'R'. Faint marks, bearing in mind it has been subject to 380 years of weathering, suggest the letter 'E' (for Elizabeth GLYD). There is no way it could be part of a letter 'J' or 'A' as has been suggested by other historians.

28

Showing the shallow flutings between arches.

The ground floor windows are recessed beneath particularly attractive brick arches. Between the windows are shallow flutings with carved brick ornamental motifs, which intrigued Sir Nikolaus PEVSNER who said on a visit: 'the oddest thing is a complete set of recessed capital in fancy brickwork. They occur in precisely the same position and shape as the pilasters themselves would have been. I know of no parallel for this anywhere in the country.'

The west side elevation.

Three 1998 photos of the hallway and staircase. At the end of the hall, beyond the staircase, were several steps leading to the rear exit door and the stairs to the basement,

directly under the main staircase. Also a photo taken by Mrs Margaret STURGE c.1967, looking out of the hallway to the sedan chair gate. (Courtesy of Derek MOORE.)

The external brickwork has attracted special attention. The mellow brick elevations seem to change colour with the late afternoon sun. This appears to be the result of the particular clay used to make the bricks. Photographers have used the effect on a number of commercial advertisements.

The overall plan provides for a room in each quadrant, with a south–north central hall leading to the stairs at the centre of the rear range.

The stone staircase is reputed to be one of the earliest examples in England of an 'open' staircase, having its steps entirely supported by the flanking walls without a central support. Sir Nikolaus PEVSNER, CBE, concluded that although some had argued that such a design could not possibly be original in a 17th-century house, 'this staircase is similar to the smaller staircase in the Queen's House at Greenwich and is undoubtedly original'. (The Queen's House was begun in 1616, stopped in 1619 when Queen Anne died, and recommenced in 1630. It was one of Inigo JONES' earliest works)

Another view of the hallway and stairs taken by Mrs Margaret STURGE c.1967. (Courtesy of Derek MOORE.)

A 2002 view of the hallway and stairs.

Celebrating an 18th birthday in 2002, with a meal in the hallway.

34

The Dining Room fireplace taken by Mrs Margaret STURGE c.1967. (Courtesy of Derek MOORE.)
(At this period the Dining Room was in the north-west quadrant, now known as the Sitting
Room.)

A handwritten note on the back of the photo below states 'Taken about 1897, before the addition of the bathrooms'. A sketch plan of the ground floor of Pendell House in the 1912 edition of H. E. MAIDEN's *Victoria County History – Surrey, Volume IV* clearly shows an extension, establishing it was built between these dates.

The rear elevation in 2017 and a stone, marked with initials I.P. and date 1832, set in the wall (at the foot of the ladder).

The row of cottages during the STURGE family occupation 1936–69 were the schoolroom, which became the playroom when the children grew out of the nursery; the gardener's cottage, with the bedrooms extending over the garage, and on the left of the garage were stables where the livestock was housed. Charlie STURGE says 'during the war we had two cows, milked by the chauffeur, to the detriment of polishing the Bentley!'

The 1832 stone.

The outline of the former garage (coach-house), now a French window, can be clearly seen. The cottages are currently named 'Holly', 'Freedom', 'Stable' and 'Mulberry' Cottages.

The stone is currently inexplicable as John PERKINS and his family were in residence at this time, but nobody with the initial 'I' has been traced.

The gardens of the adjacent cottages.

North rear elevation showing the 1897/1912 extension and the exit from the main corridor.

Steps leading to the basement oil store on the west elevation, facing Pendell Road.

North rear elevation looking west in 1999, showing lean-to, with the row of cottages now behind a dividing wall.

The Library (now known as the Drawing Room) fireplace, in the south-west quadrant taken by Mrs Margaret STURGE c.1967. (Courtesy of Derek MOORE.)

The Dining Room (now known as the Sitting Room) in the north-west quadrant taken by Mrs Margaret STURGE c.1967. (Courtesy of Derek MOORE.)

The original dining room oak table, said to be 300 years old and left with the house when the STURGE family sold Pendell House in 1969. Taken by Mrs Margaret STURGE c.1967. (Courtesy of Derek MOORE) It was regarded as 'a friend of the family' having been saved when the then Dining Room (now the Sitting Room) was damaged by fire in 1937.

Three views of the Drawing Room in the south-west quadrant. The bottom photo shows the window that turns into a raised door, leading to the garden.

Adjacent Sitting Room in the north-west quadrant.

Dining Room in south-east quadrant in 1999, before alteration.

In 2002 after enlargement, exposing the fireplace and removing the kitchen pantry.

The kitchen in 1998, with old tiling and Aga.

In 2001, after modernisation.

FIRST FLOOR

The first and second floor arrangements repeat those on the ground floor, i.e. four main heated rooms in each quadrant.

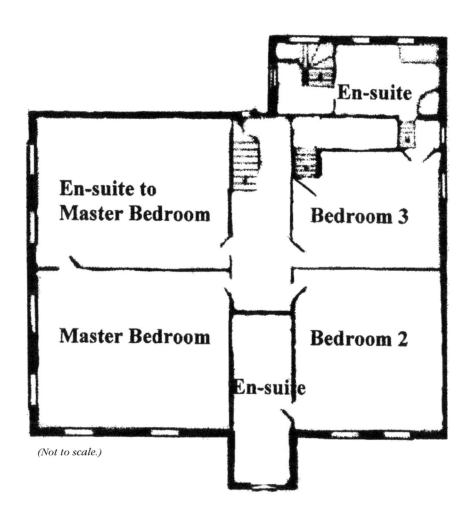

En-suite

En-suite to Master Bedroom

Bedroom 3

Master Bedroom

Bedroom 2

En-suite

(Not to scale.)

During the occupancy of the STURGE family (1936–1969) the Master Bedroom was the Children's Room and the En-Suite to the Master Bedroom was the Nursery. Bedroom 2 was the Nurse's room and Bedroom 3 was the Master Bedroom.

Master bedroom on the first floor south-west quadrant.

The adjoining former bedroom in the north-west quadrant, now converted to a large en-suite for the Master bedroom.

The original en-suite to the Master bedroom, as it was when the house was purchased in 1997 and prior to the conversion as en-suite of the adjacent new bedroom 2.

Now modernised as the en-suite for the new bedroom 2.

SECOND FLOOR

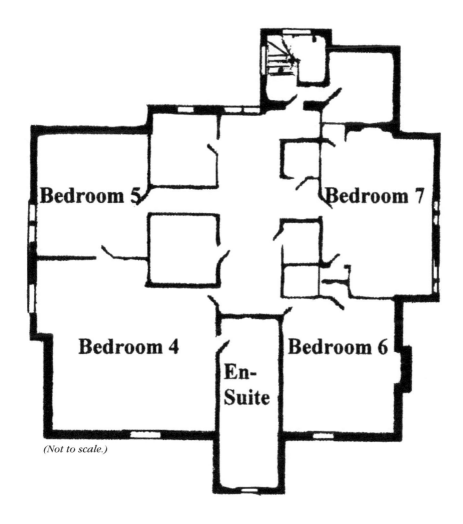

Bedroom 5

Bedroom 7

Bedroom 4

En-
Suite

Bedroom 6

(Not to scale.)

On the second floor the hallway and several of the rooms are lined with 17th-century wainscot panelling. It can be seen in the lower wall of the above two photos.

Although there are references to the panelling coming from Pendell Court in settlement of a debt, it may be that these have been moved from the lower floors when the house was renovated in the 18th century. Such changes might have been carried out 1747–1803 when the JELFE family were resident.

Bedroom 4.

Of the four chimney stacks, two rise in the flank walls to heat the front rooms and two rise in the rear wall in the north to heat the rear rooms. Of the two on the garden side of the west elevation, one bears the inscription R E, with G over the top, and the date 1636. A local historian suggested this was erected by John GLYD, the bachelor son of Richard, and bears his initials and that of his mother, Anne.

Bedroom 5.

Bedroom 7 in the north-east quadrant (used by the author and his wife on many occasions), showing the same 17th-century wainscot panelling.

It was thought that perhaps the chimney had been struck by lightning, or somehow damaged, and had to be rebuilt following the same design.

The author disagrees with this theory, it does not make sense for the date 1636 to be placed on the second chimney if it was constructed post 1666, when 16-year-old John GLYD inherited the house with his mother Anne. What is much more likely is that the initials were those of Richard and Elizabeth GLYD's surviving children. They had lost seven children, two daughters, both called Mary, and five sons, two called Abraham, two Charles and a John by 1635, so their four surviving children in 1636 were precious to them.

Close-up of the inscription R G E 1636 on the south-east chimney facing the garden.

49

The surviving children in 1636 were John, aged 19 (1617–1638); Richard, aged 18 (1618–1658); Elizabeth aged 4 (1632–1661) (who married William BEWLEY and later Richard CHANDLER) and Anne, aged 2, b.1634 (who married William WRIGHT). It therefore makes sense that their surviving four beloved children were commemorated by the initials JGA and RGE in the chimneys erected towards the end of 1636.

It was a tragedy that John died only two years later. Because of their condition the chimneys were rebuilt in 1959 but although the original initials R E with G over the top, and date 1636 were retained on one chimney, there is now no J G A visible on any chimney. Charlie STURGE recalls that the builder was a Mr MAYNARD, who never presented a bill!

The chimneypieces in the royal closet above the gallery in the Queen's Chapel are of a type that JONES popularised, a pedimented overmantel above a chimney surround. There are numerous references to JONES re-drawing chimney piece designs with one drawn in January 1636, the same year that Pendell House was completed. Inigo also designed the chimneypieces for the Cabinet Room in the Queen's House in 1637 and one for Somerset House, again in 1636.

The original marble fireplaces are also worthy of mention, with the chimney flues large enough for a small boy to climb up, as no doubt happened.

Other marble fireplaces in the house are similar, with variations in their design.

4. THE GARDEN & GROUNDS

Drastic changes have taken place since Pendell House was first built. This 1891 Ordnance Survey map shows how the track (running diagonally from the bottom left of the walled garden) leading to Ockley Farm, less than a mile away, can be seen and how the grounds extended a considerable distance (sold with 40 acres in 1695).

An enlarged section, showing the garden layout in 1891 (note no rear extension) The four cottages to the immediate north of the house are coach houses and servants' quarters.

But this sketch shows how the construction of the M23 not only reduced the grassland grounds to 13 acres but removed the real need for the public footpath No. 172, which was obliterated by the M23 and now merely leads back to the upper part of Pendell Road.

The garden facing the west elevation, showing the old Dew Pond. All taken by Mrs Margaret STURGE c.1967. (Courtesy of Derek MOORE.)

From the west in 1997.

The dramatic changes to the garden layout were carried out by two lady gardeners, Judy and Gaye. They were not only expert in their field but worked tirelessly to carry out the transformation

Over time they became close personal friends of the family.

The lower garden in 1998.

Landscaping almost complete 1999.

In full bloom 2001.

Swimming pool, converted from the Old Dew pond. Taken by Mrs Margaret STURGE c.1967. (Courtesy of Derek MOORE.)

The swimming pool and changing room 1997.

Showing the entrance in the north wall to the tennis court and greenhouse.

The tennis court 1999.

The croquet lawn pre-1920, now the site of the greenhouse and sheds. (Courtesy of Derek MOORE.)

Garden sheds and greenhouse, beyond the north wall.

Inside the north wall in 1997, heavily overgrown.

North wall cleared and with pergola constructed – 1999.

The completed pergola, showing screen of very tall trees shielding the tennis court in the background.

The herbaceous border on the north wall, 150 yards long and said to be one of the finest in the country. (The grotto can just be seen at the end.) Both above photos taken by Mrs Margaret STURGE c.1967. (Courtesy of Derek MOORE.)

Grotto, believed built by Andrews JELFE, in north-west corner of garden.

There is a subterraneous passage, 4ft wide by 6ft high, excavated on the south wall 112ft from the house. It currently extends 97ft towards the riverbed below, ending where the dry stone roof has collapsed. Entry is no longer sensible due to Health & Safety considerations, plus the fact that protected species bats use it as a hibernation site. One school of thought was that it was built as a means of escape, exiting near the stream at the south-east corner of the property, possibly built during the

Steps and gate, possibly built by Andrews JELFE c.1897.

Civil War. Another suggestion is that an owner built it to gain access to a mistress in the Pendhill area.

The author rejects both theories. Pendell House is not a structure that is easily defended and any escape tunnel would surely have been dug from the south end of the basement. The tunnel is also very conspicuous, although the brick built steps and iron gate were almost certainly constructed at a later period. To gain access to a mistress without the wife knowing also does not stand up to scrutiny, because she would have been well aware of the tunnel.

The tunnel was discovered in 1897 by Andrews JELFE's gardener when he cut down some trees. It was then 210ft long, with a bricked roof and walls. An outside roof access point, 23ft from the garden wall, is now covered by a concrete slab.

Although there is a small ice-house in the south-west corner of the basement, it is more likely that the tunnel was used as the main ice-house, the ice coming from the lake or dew pond at either end. When ice is packed together, its relatively small surface area slows down the thawing process. Ice will, of course, last longer if kept at a regular low temperature and insulated by straw, thick walls and a roof.

Ice houses tend to be located close to a water source, such as a lake, in order to easily harvest ice in the depths of winter. (It should be noted that the Pendell House tunnel had a lake at each end.) Ice houses also have a drain hole in the base for the slow-melting ice to drain away. In the case of the Pendell House ice-house it could have drained into the lower lake, but a full ice house could take up to 18 months to thaw.

Ice was used in France at the end of the 16th century but in England it seems storing ice was introduced at the time of the Restoration by Royalists, who had been in exile on the Continent during the time of the Commonwealth. An early reference to ice-houses being built was in October 1660, in Upper St James Park, now known as Green Park:

> *The icehouse forms an excellent store Larder for the preservation of every kind of food liable to be injured by heat in summer; and for the table, where coolness is desirable, the use of ice in summer is a great luxury.*

J. B. Papworth, 1819

The following pictures of icehouses in Hampshire gardens are similar to that in the garden of Pendell House. *(All four photos are Courtesy of and © Hampshire Industrial Archaeology Society)*

Stratton Park, Micheldever.

Arnewood House, Hordle, built 1832.

Idsworth House, Kingsworthy.

Fairfield House, Hambledon.

Pendell Road. The Pound, for stray animals, was on the left, where it was all open common up to the Reigate Road. Photo on right shows where the 1906 entrance was located. Both taken by Mrs Margaret STURGE c.1967. (Courtesy of Derek MOORE.)

The start of building a renewed main entrance gate to the house, 1999.

The final construction of the electrically controlled gate, at the main entrance to the property. Designed to be in keeping with the remainder of the walls.

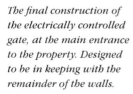

Entrance, high enough to accommodate a sedan chair, and scalloped wall creating a courtyard, also believed built by Andrews JELFE. The drive was refurbished in 1999.

Construction of a sewerage treatment plant that also served the row of cottages at the rear (at no cost to them) c.1999.

The lake in the south of the property, with an island containing shelters to safeguard the ducks from marauding foxes.

Taken from the bund, showing part of the acreage outside the walled garden.

The walled garden of Pendell House has a well-proportioned scalloped wall, with piers, at the extreme west of the walled garden. This curtain wall was built by Andrews JELFE *c.*1750 on an original, much older sunken brick wall that was probably contemporary with the house. If so, it could have been a 'ha-ha' wall 80 years before the word 'ha-ha' was known.

A 'ha ha' was a hidden boundary, a sunken wall, separating park from garden on an estate. Its installation prevented livestock from encroaching on the more elegant part of the estate. It kept nature at a respectful distance. You could still view your land from your house, but the inhabitants would not bother you. The name 'ha-ha' may derive from the unexpected (i.e., amusing) moment of discovery when, on approach from the rear, the vertical drop suddenly becomes visible.

Another example of a 'ha-ha' can be found at the nearby Old Rectory in Brewer Street, Blechingley, near another old ice house.

Garden

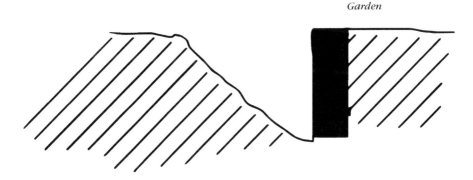

A 'ha-ha' wall.

Demolishing the by now derelict wall c.1998 and carefully rebuilding it.

67

Fully completed by 2000.

The south wall, raised walkway inside, a full rabbit warren in 1999.

Martin's Pond, on the southern portion of the estate. It was filled in with old lorry and car tyres by 'Paddy' MARTIN, together with waste rubble, and is now under the M23 motorway. (Courtesy of Derek MOORE.)

Directly opposite Pendell House, in the main road, Pendell Road, is George Holman's larger 1624 Pendell Court, built of red brick with stone mullioned windows, tiled roof, marble fireplaces and original panelling and staircase. It has been used as the main building of a private school, The Hawthorns Preparatory School (ages 2–13) since 1961.

5. TIME LINE OF OCCUPANTS & EVENTS

This shows the dates when occupants are either known or believed to be occupants, and particular events involving Pendell House, Blechingley or the country. Ownership and occupation of Pendell House did not always coincide and it was often difficult to distinguish between the two, but where it is believed that the occupant was only renting, this is made clear in the text.

1367
The place name of PENDHILL is first found in Sir Thomas UVEDALE's Will.

1451
A house in Blechingley was held by a John Schriches, Opposite was an old cross with an open area nearby, together with the village pound where unclaimed animals were kept. The cross was probably the market cross of Pendell, which never became a proper market.

1455
Henry VI, king from 1422 until he was deposed in 1461, started the War of the Roses, two years after the Hundred Years War ended.

1483
13-year-old Edward V, and his brother Prince Richard, were murdered in the Tower of London. This ended the War of the Roses, with Richard III becoming king.

1495
Pendell House almost certainly stands on the site of the holding known as Schryches, after John Scriche (or sometimes Skerrett) whose family still held it in 1495 (the name of the householder is the same as that in 1451). At this time, the labelling of houses with a name was still rare and even many decades later people were content that their houses should be known by their owner's name.

1520

The Pendell market cross was described as 'now decayed'.

1540

Anne of Cleves was given Blechingley by Henry VIII (king from 1509–1547).

1547

Blechingley passed to Sir Thomas Cawarden, a keen Reformer, when Anne of Cleves became the owner of Richmond Palace and Hever Castle. After Elizabeth came to the throne in 1558, Sir Thomas Cawarden fell out of favour and died in the Tower in 1559. He is buried on the right-hand side of Blechingley Church High Altar.

THE GLYD FAMILY

The GLYD crest is described as:

> *On a bend between 3 annulets, 6 fleur-de-lys 2, 2 & 2 and 2 crosses crosslet, a label of 3 points for difference, impaling a cross engrailed ermine.*
> *A griffin sejeant the Dexter for paws elevated wings elevated and plain collared and lines gu Under the hands of Clarence Cooke, King of Arms.*

It is believed that it was awarded to Richard GLYD (1505–1567) of Brightling, Sussex.

(Drawn by and courtesy of Sue DOWN)

Richard GLYD (1548–1618) of Brightling, Sussex (where the family had been settled for three generations) married Martha (1556–1619), daughter of Edward SCOTESFORD of Bransby, Kent, 3 February 1578.

Richard inherited the lease on the property Weard, or Worth as it later became, in West Sussex, from his father, Thomas GLYD, and lived there with his wife Martha from 1604 to 1618, until he died on 5 April at Brightling, Sussex. Richard then followed the irksome habit of successive generations of a family bearing the same Christian name, making life difficult for family historians.

1605

James I of England and VI of Scotland was the first king to rule over England and Scotland. His rule was marked by the Gunpowder Plot, when Guy Fawkes and his friends decided to blow up the Houses of Parliament.

1610

Richard GLYD's status can be gleaned from a Deed Poll of Surrender held in the National Archives, dated 15 December, which states:

> *By Richard Glyd of Werth in Brightling, yeoman, servant to Robert, Lord Sidney of Penhurst, Viscount Lisle, Lord Governor of Flushing and Lord Chamberlain to the Queen, to Robert Viscount Lisle of a Lease by the said Viscount dated 10 Dec. 2 Jas 1 of the Manor or farm called Weard also Werth and one tenement or dwelling house with barns, stable and edifaces belonging, And two watermills called Wythamfor Mills and all closes lands, meadow, pasture, arables and rough land, waters bays and banks to the said Manor or farm, tenements and mills belonging All which manor, farm, lands and premises containing 530 acres, whereof one acre belonging to Wythamford lay in Burwash and the residue in Brightling. Signature Richard Glyd, Witnesses – Chr Milles, Ernott, Edwn Taylor.*

In 1617, he purchased the Manor of Worth *in its entirety,* including house, bar, stables, 500 acres, two water mills called Wythaford Mills for £1,600. (Worth Village is in West Sussex, within the neighbourhood of Pound Hill in the Borough of Crawley.)

1617

The Manor of Pendhill, with its 310 acres, was purchased from John TYNDALL by George HOLMAN, grocer of London, whose family had lived for many years in Godstone.

The Pilgrim Fathers sailed to America in the Mayflower.

1624

Neighbouring Pendell Court was built by George HOLMAN, who died the following year and his son Robert, a Barrister, inherited the Manor. He was a Puritan who supported Parliament in the later Civil War. It was in this house that for generations the Lords of the Manor, or their Stewards, held regular courts. Tenants were obliged to attend and do 'fealty' and manorial laws were enforced. The Lord of the Manor settled disputes and punished criminals.

1625

Charles I, the son of James I and Anne of Denmark, came to the throne. He believed that he ruled by divine right and this caused difficulties with Parliament from the outset.

1633

Richard GLYD (1587–1666), a wealthy Tallow Chandler, the second son of Richard GLYD (1548–1618) started to build 'Pendell', or 'Glyd's house' or 'late Schriches', as it was often alluded to. He had inherited a considerable sum from his father's estate and was described as 'good, prudent, wise and pious'. His father had been Apprentice to wealthy Tallow Chandler William EVANS and later became his partner. ('Tallow Chandler' meant he dealt in candles made from tallow, i.e. animal fat.)

Richard GLYD had married Elizabeth EVANS (1590–1672) 14 October 1612 at Brightling, Sussex. She was the niece of William EVANS, who had died in 1611 and was the late partner of Richard. Elizabeth was also the daughter of Charles EVANS, whose father David EVANS seems to have been the first EVANS to settle in Blechingley, after marrying Ann GILMYN from Reigate.

Richard had become a Governor of Christ's Church Hospital in 1627 and was their Treasurer from 1652 to 1662. He also purchased a large burial plot for 23 bodies in St Mary the Virgin Churchyard, Blechingley.

1636

Pendell House was completed and Richard GLYD (1587–1666), also became Master of his Tallow Chandlers Company (and again in 1639). Although there is no firm evidence, there is every reason to believe that the house was built on top of what was the basement of John Schriches house, that may have become derelict. The basement of Pendell House therefore possibly dates from before 1451.

Inigo JONES.

The factors governing the belief that Inigo JONES was involved in the construction of Pendell House, possibly by supplying plans, are:

(1) A rigidly symmetrically layout, typical of Jones.

(2) The staircase identical to and contemporary with the Queens House, built by Inigo at the same time as Pendell.

(3) The chimney stacks, something that Inigo was in the habit of designing.

(4) The sash windows thought to be original and ahead of their time.

Richard's brother-in-law, Thomas EVANS, had bought an estate in Blechingley in 1627 and was living at Hall House in the village, so Richard brought his wife home to her own people when he built Pendell in 1636 and settled here.

Plaques (Appendix A) in Blechingley's St Mary the Virgin Church reveal the rapid christenings and burials that seemed especially marked for the short-lived GLYD and EVANS families.

According to one church plaque, Richard and Elizabeth had at least 11 children, John (1617–1638), Richard (1618–1658), Abraham (1627–1635), Mary (1629–1630), second Mary (b&d late 1630), Charles (1631–1635), Elizabeth (1632) married William MERRICKS 1660, and Ann (1634) married William WRIGHT. A further Abraham, Charles and John on the plaque could not be traced in the baptism records.

NB: Mary GLYD is recorded in the St Mary the Virgin Church, Blechingley, parish records as being buried there 8 June 1630, 'daughter of Richard Glyd of London'. The GLYD family thus had a foothold in Blechingley well before Richard started to build Pendell House.

Blechingley – A Parish History states:

> *The third house at Pendell, once known as 'Little Pendhill' but of recent years christened, without a shadow of historical justification,*

'The Manor House', stands at the foot of Pendell Hill, divided from the Court grounds only by its own shrubberies and the ornamental water. It is a red brick gabled house, 'said to have been built by Richard Glyd Esq., as a temporary residence whilst he was building his other house', according to Manning and 'dating from the early eighteenth century' according to the Victoria County History.

Both statements are probably untrue: the first because it is incredible a man should build a 'temporary residence' not such a very great deal smaller than the permanent one he was engaged in erecting a short distance away; the second because the oldest part of the house clearly dates from long before the eighteenth century.

1642

The outbreak of the English Civil War, which lasted four years. St Paul's Cathedral was already in severe structural decline by the 17th century and restoration work started by Inigo Jones in the 1620s was halted by the Civil War.

1646

Following the defeat of the Royalist forces by the New Model Army, led by Oliver Cromwell, King Charles was captured and imprisoned.

1649

The House of Commons tried King Charles for treason and he was convicted and beheaded on 30 January. The British monarchy was then abolished and a Republic called 'The Commonwealth of England' declared.

It was during this period that Richard GLYD, who supported the Commonwealth, served in the politically sensitive role of Common Councilman in the City.

A document in the National Archives, dated 1 November, details a lease for a year by Richard GLYD, citizen and Mercer of London, to Nicholas STOUGHTON, Robert PURSE of Worplesdon in Surrey, gent., Richard WITHER of Stoke next to Guildford, Surrey, gent and Henry BALDWYN, Gent, of Guildford. (Richard GLYD is thus trying to raise money by means of the lease, having erected Pendell House, then called Shriches.)

The property was described as:

One mansion house called Shriches, all barns, stables and gardens and commons and lands called Shriches croft, Reerecroft, Bramley croft, Battsfield, Battesmede containing 14a in all near Pendhill near Bletchingley in Surrey in occupation of Richard Glyd the 3rd, also all messuage and tenement barn and orchard, garden and two crofts of land belonging containing 3a called Coneys, 16a in Bletchingley in occupation of Henry Burton and all that is Weard in Brightling; one messuage, two barns, one outhouse called Shephouse or Waynhouse, land called Holtscroft and two crofts, part of upper woods and beechfields and 18a, the upper Malling, the pilrede, three fields called Ashreeds upper and lower, Bramblefield, little meadows, homefields, large woods and Ryecroft.

1653

Oliver Cromwell expelled the corrupt English parliament and with the agreement of army leaders became Lord Protector of the Commonwealth of England, Scotland and Ireland.

1654

Robert HOLMAN, Barrister, of nearby Pendell Court, became one of six local MPs elected to the first Protectorate Parliament. He was therefore clearly a Parliamentarian, not a Royalist.

1658

Oliver Cromwell died from natural causes and was buried in Westminster Abbey. His son, Richard, then became Lord Protector but resigned after nine months, going abroad where he lived in relative obscurity until he returned in 1680.

1660

The army and parliament then asked the son of Charles I to take the throne. Although popular and known as 'The Merry Monarch', Charles II was a weak king and had 13 known mistresses, one of whom was Nell Gwyn. When the Royalists returned to power they had Oliver Cromwell's body dug up, hung in chains and beheaded.

Richard GLYD (1587-1666), was certainly heavily involved in City politics as a supporter of the Presbyterians but it appears his true loyalties were to the Royalist cause. He was one of the three Treasurers of the loan raised to finance the disbandment of the New Model Army.

1661

The Hearth-tax returns record that 'Mr Richard Glyde's house' was actually bigger than that of Robert Holman Esq, (i.e. Pendell Court on the opposite side of the road), having 18 hearths against his 16.

1665

The Great Plague, the last major epidemic of the bubonic plague to occur in England, started and lasted for over a year.

1666

Richard GLYD (1587–1666) the builder of Pendell House, died and under his Will, 276 acres of his land in Brightling were leased to his sons-in-law, Richard CHANDLER, citizen and haberdasher of London and William WRIGHT, cloth worker of London. Richard was buried in the south chapel of St Mary the Virgin Church, Blechingley. His son Richard (1618–1658), had followed a business career like his father, at New Shoreham, Sussex. A token, inscribed 'Richard Glyd of New' with RGA in the centre was found. (The solitary 'New' clearly related to New Shoreham.) The 'A' was his wife's initial, Ann (1630–1711), daughter of Anthony STOUGHTON of Worplesdon, who he married c. 1649. Ann's brother was Sir Nicholas STOUGHTON of Guildford.

As Richard (1618–1658) had died, his eldest son **John GLYD** (1650–1689), at the age of 16, thus inherited the property in 1666, together with his mother Ann. He also inherited the property called Little Worge, Brightling, Sussex, but as he was underage custody was granted to his mother Ann.

The Great Fire of London swept through the centre of London from Sunday, 2 September to Wednesday, 5 September 1666. It destroyed 13,200 houses and St Paul's Cathedral. After demolition of the old structure, the present, domed cathedral was erected on the site, with an English Baroque design by Wren.

John GLYD matriculated 12 July 1666, entered St Edmund Hall, Oxford University, and became a Barrister at Gray's Inn in 1674.

1672

Elizabeth GLYD, wife of Richard GLYD (1587–1666), died in Blechingley at the age of 82. Her Will read as follows:

Will of Elizabeth GLYD

In the name of God Amen, I, Elizabeth Glyd, wider, of the parish of Blechingley Gentily bein very weak and full of greif for my decayed husband yet in perfect understanding & memory do think fit to make my will & do give unto to my only childe Ann Wright wife of William Wright all my goods plate household stuff linen pewter brass beddin wearin cloaths & all my money only such as I shall dispose of as followeth to her daughter Ann Wright my Granddaughter the summe of fifty pounds to my Grandaughter Blanche Wright the summe of fifty pounds to my grand sonn William Wright the summe of fifty pounds all the rest of my moneys plate cloathe goods whatsoever to be hers & to be for her one use and comfort while she lives or to deliver all it to the rest of her children as she shall see good & her husband not to have the profit or use of the moneys but she for her owne good & the good of her children that whatsoever is mine should be hers and her children.

On the 27th March in the yeare of our Lorde 1666 I have here to set my hand and seale - - - - EG   Sealed and delivered in the presence Fudetkauens.

Ann Evans

The first St Mary the Virgin Church churchwarden's book records entries from 1672 to 1676 for a collection to help other areas suffering from fires. In this 'John Glyd Esq. and his mother, Anne Glid, widd., each gave 5s'.

1681
Charles II dissolved the English Parliament and ruled alone until his death.

1685
Charles II died on 6 February and was received into the Roman Catholic Church on his deathbed.

He was succeeded by James II of England and VII of Scotland, the second surviving son of Charles I and younger brother of Charles II.

1688

James was generally hated because of his persecution of the Protestant clergy and the Bloody Assizes of Judge Jeffries. Parliament then asked the Dutch Prince William of Orange to take the throne. William, full name William Henry Stuart, was the son of William II and Mary Stuart, the eldest daughter of Charles I. On 5 November, William of Orange sailed his fleet of over 450 ships into Torbay harbour and landed his troops. Gathering local support, he marched his army of 20,000 to London whilst many of James II's army defected to support William, as well as James' other daughter, Anne.

1689

John GLYD (1650–1689) became the MP for Blechingley on 14 January 1689, died 23 November the same year, unmarried, and was buried at St Mary the Virgin Church, Blechingley, 29 November. A black marble gravestone, within the altar rails of St Mary the Virgin Church, Blechingley, bears the inscription, in capitals:

> *Here lyeth the body of John Glid, late of Pendhill in this parish, Esquire, Barrister at Law of the Society of Grayes Inn, and one of the Burgesses for the Borough of Blechingley in the first parliament of theire Majesties King William and Queene Mary, who departed this life the 22nd day of November 1689.*

John GLYD'S Will, dated 15 November 1689, only a week before his death, opened with the request to Samuel WESTERNE Esq. 'to keepe by him that will of mine which he has in his custody and not to inspect it unless this my present will be contested, then I would have him show the same to the parties contending, that they may see what they are likely to get by overthrowing this present will.' As a Lawyer he thus intended to thwart any attempt to contest the Will by having an earlier Will that would come into effect if his final Will was overturned.

He left his 'capital messuage called Pendhill, with the farm 'Pigeons Land' let to Robert Wooden and the farm at Warwick Wood for life, unto my loving mother Mrs Ann Glyd for the terme of her life and after her decease to my sister Anne Glyd'. His sister Ann was also to have, at once, the house at Pendhill occupied by **Mr Richard STREATE** *(Nothing is known of Richard STREATE)* with land belonging; a farm called Highfield and a house and barn on the north side of the churchyard. John GLYD also left 10 shillings to his cousin Richard GLYD of Darlington and 5 shillings to each of Richard's children.

His Sussex lands at Brightling and Burwash were left equally between his two sisters, Martha DRAKE and Ann GLYD, charged with a payment of £100 apiece to Martha's children, Ralph, Anne and Martha DRAKE.

His mother Anne was sole executrix and residuary legatee and was charged to 'bury me privately in Blechingley chancel, to have only a herse and the necessary charges, having always been of opinion against the superfluous expenses of funerals'.

The poor of Blechingley were left £25; twenty 'most intimate friends' were to have gold rings worth 15 shillings apiece; each of his cousin Sir Nicholas STOUGHTON's children a ring value £1; £10 to his cousin Richard GLYD of Dallington and £5 apiece to his children. His servants Walter and Roger were given £2, and £1 each to his mother's three maidservants. His mother had to burn all his manuscripts, books and papers, except 'what related to other people's concerns' and his friend Joseph NEWINGTON was to have 'Rolls his grand abridgement in 4 vols.'

Ann GLYD (1632–1711) thus became the owner of Pendell House, and after her decease John's sister Anne, but it is thought that neither of them ever lived there. (Ann GLYD's daughter, Anne, had married William BROCKMAN so it is assumed they never lived in Pendell House, having possibly rented it to John AMHERST.)

Ann Glyd (1632–1711) died in 1711 and her Will read as follows:

Will of Ann GLYD read in April 1713 at Blechingley
30 November 1703

In the name of God Amen in the second year of our Soverain Lady Queen Ann Defender of the Faith By the Grace of God of England Scotland France and Ireland and in the year of our Lord one thousand seven hundred and three John Glyd widow of the parish of Blechingly in the County of Surrey Being In pretty good health but in sound understanding Doe now make my Last Will and doe Hereby Revoke all former wills

To God my heavenly Father I commit my soul in whose alone mercy through the merits and mediation of his only son and my alone saviour I trust to enjoy Everlasting Life and happyness

My body I desire to be Desently Burryed In the Chancel of Bletchingley Church in the Grave of my Son John Glyd under His Gravestone and of concerning the Disposition of that Estate that my God hath Gratiously Given me I Dispose it In Manner and Form Following

I Give three pound Lawful English mony to the poor of the parish of Bletchingley To Be Distributed amongst them that Day my Funeral sermons preached

I will and devise To my Granddaughter Mrs Ann Drake and to my GrandDaughter Mrs Martha Drake Being Both of them of the parrish of Blechingley in Surrey and to the survivors of them and their Assigns all Thos my parcels of Land arable meadow and pastuer with the appurtances commonly called or known by the name of or name of Highfeilds and Highfeild mead containing by Estimation thirteen acres more or less lying and Being in the parish of Bletchingley afforsaid now in the tenure or occupation of John Russel

Upon the several and Respective Trusts hearafter Following that is to say that the said Estate Be to my Grandson John Drake son of Ralph Drake late of Bletchingley afforesaid Gentleman Deceased since He attains the age of one and Twenty years and Thenceforth to him and his heirs for Ever Charged nevertheless with the Respective sumes of Thirty pound apiece

To Granddaughters Elizabeth and Sarah Drake Daughters of the said Ralph Drake deceased to be paid to them at their Respective ages of nineteen years and that in the meantime my said Trusties Doe Receive the Rents dues and profits of the said Estate and doe pay and account for the same in Manner following that is to say for one moyety therof to my said Grandson John Drake on his attaining his age of one and Twenty years and for one fourth part therof to each of my said too Granddaughters making Together the other royaty at their Respective ages of nineteen years

But in case the said John Drake dye before his age of one and twenty years my will and mind is that the Estate itself shall be and the mean profitts therof shall be paid By my said Trusties to and Between my Granddaughters and their heirs Respectively and in case Either of my too Granddaughters dye before her age of ninteen years without Issue Then her part and share of the said Estate and the profitt therof shall remain and be paid to the surviving sister and her heirs forever and in case Both the said sisters dye before Nineteen years of age without issue then the whole Estate from the said Charge with the profits therof soley and wholely to the said John Drake and his heirs for Ever provided always and my will is that if either of my said Grandchildren Leave and Issue of his or her Body lawfully Begotten at Their Respective Deaths aforesaid that then such issue shall have and injoy the Mothers or Fathers part and share of the Estate and Profitts therof afore mentioned

Ann Glyd

The Heighfeilds mentioned in the Will is probably today's Highfields in the Sandhills Parkland, a small hamlet located between the villages of Wormley and Brook. It is part of the Surrey Hills Area of Outstanding Beauty and situated on the Greensand Way. There is a Common owned by the National Trust, and a Donkey sanctuary, founded by John and Kay Lockwood in the 1950s and now operated by the RSPCA on the site.

Of the two beneficiaries mentioned in the Will, Anne's granddaughter, Ann DRAKE, widow, was buried at Blechingley on 5 April, 1766, and her other granddaughter, Martha DRAKE, was buried there 2 February 1768.

THE AMHERST FAMILY

1690
William III defeated James and French troops at the Battle of the Boyne in Ireland and James fled to France as guest of Louis XIV, and died in exile in 1701. It was decided that William III and Mary II would reign jointly and for William III to have the crown for life.

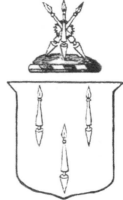

The Bill of Rights was also passed to establish the order of succession for Mary II's heirs. It stipulated that no Catholic could succeed to the throne, and also limited the powers of the Royal prerogative. The King or Queen could not withhold laws passed by Parliament or levy taxes without Parliamentary consent.

John AMHERST (1618–1691), from Horsmonden, Kent, purchased Pendell House in 1690 but only owned it for a year, dying in Sevenoaks, Kent, in 1691 and buried 9 May in St Michael's, Mickleham, Dorking, Surrey.

John had matriculated to St John's College, University of Oxford, 19 May 1637, where he gained his BA and attained Barrister-at-Law at Gray's Inn in 1646. He was the Treasurer of Gray's Inn 1673–75.

He had married three times, first to Margaret KIRBY, 4 January 1648, the mother of his son Jeffrey; second to Elizabeth TRIGGS, who died 1667; and thirdly, to Lady Jane ONSLOW, daughter of Sir Francis STYDOLPHE and widow of Sir Henry ONSLOW, on 10 November 1668. Jane was buried at Mickleham, 20 September 1684.

It is thought that John AMHERST possibly rented Pendell House some time prior to purchasing it, because his son Jeffrey had married Elizabeth YATE, the granddaughter of Sir Francis STYDOLPHE of Mickleham, in Blechingley, 8 October 1670. They also had a son there, Henry, born 17 January 1676, who sadly died the following day.

Another factor strengthening an earlier renting is that the Blechingley Parliamentary Record states 'The other Member returned at the General Election, John Glyd, owned property in the parish, though he lived in Chambers at Gray's Inn.' John GLYD, of course, was single, so when he inherited Pendell House in 1666 at the age of 16 it would have been too large for him, with no family of his own.

Also, the first St Mary the Virgin churchwarden's book records entries from 1672 to 1676 for a collection to help other areas suffering from fires. It includes an entry of 5s given by John Amherst Esq.

John AMHERST had two brothers, also from Horsmonden, Kent, who also obtained University of Oxford degrees and attended the same St John's College. (1) Richard AMHERST, who matriculated 27 June 1634, obtained his BA 31 January 1637/8 and became Rector of Southease, Sussex in 1642. (2) Arthur AMHERST, who matriculated 19 May 1637, obtained BA 28 January 1640/1, D.Med. 11 November 1662, practised at Hastings, Sussex and Tunbridge, Kent, where he died 2 July 1678.

1691

John's son, **Jeffrey AMHERST,** born 17 April 1654, inherited Pendell House on the death of his father. He had also taken GLYD's vacant Blechingley seat in Parliament, 9 December 1689. He only held it for two months and on trying to regain the seat in the new Parliament, on 24 February 1690, only obtained 22 votes, against 241 for Thomas HOWARD and 33 for Sir Robert CLAYTON, who were both returned as MPs. Blechingley was, of course, a 'Rotten Borough' and a perfect example of a handful of eligible voters being able to return two Members of Parliament.

Jeffrey's wife, Elizabeth, had died in 1686 and he had married again by Licence from the Archbishop in Pembury, Bromley, on 4 May 1687 to Dorothy CRADOCK, who died 4 May 1712, a year before Jeffrey.

The AMHERST family went on to greater things. Jeffery AMERST'S grandson, also Jeffrey, became Field Marshall and was raised to the peerage on 14 May 1776, as Baron Amherst of Holmesdale in the County of Kent. On 24 March 1778 he was promoted to full General and, in April 1778, he became Commander-in-Chief of the Forces, which gave him a seat in the Cabinet. He was also the first British Governor General of the Territories that eventually became Canada. He died 3 August 1797.

His brother, William AMHERST, was Aide-de-Camp to King George III and Lieut. Governor of Newfoundland. He died 13 May 1781.

1694

Queen Mary II died of smallpox and William III ruled alone until he died in 1702.

THE PELLATT FAMILY

1695

WILLIAM PELLATT (II) (*c.*1650–1722) with his wife Elizabeth, purchased Pendell House between February and October that year from Jeffrey AMHERST. The Pellatts were an old Sussex family from Steyning, where Richard PELLATT was MP in 1572.

(The 1,100 acres estate Park and Manor of Bignor were held from at least the mid-fourteenth century by the Earls of Arundel. Originally used as grounds to fatten deer, Bignor Park was bought in 1584 by Richard Pellatt, MP, who built the first house on the site, the only surviving relics of which are two finials at the west end of the walled garden. The property descended through his family until sold by William Pellatt (II) in 1712 to Nicholas Turner.)

The PELLATT Family Crest. A lion passant ermine, holding in the lion's dexter paw an oak branch proper.

The PELLATT family also followed the habit of successive generations bearing the same Christian name. William's father, also William PELLATT (I) of Bignor, 'ironmonger, citizen and grocer of London', had married Mary, née HARGREAVE and widow of Thomas WOOD, in 1666. Mary died in 1697 and was buried in West Heathly. William PELLATT (I) died 11 June 1700 aged 73 and his only son and executor, William PELLATT (II), buried him at Blechingley on 28 June that year. William's (I) Will, made 12 June 1699 and proved 2 July 1700, made no mention of Blechingley, but left 40 shillings 'to the poor of Bignor' and stated 'I desire to be decently buried'.

William (II), who had become High Sherriff of Bignor Park in 1688, and Elizabeth already had four children baptised at East Grinstead, two sons, William (III), baptised 20 January 1693, Edward baptised 22 July 1694, and two daughters, Elizabeth, baptised 8 September 1689 and Mary, baptised 7 May 1691. Thomas was baptised at St Mary's, Blechingley that October, 1695. However, Elizabeth had been buried at East Grinstead on 14 February that year so it would appear that she died there in giving birth to Thomas, hence he was not baptised until October, after they moved to Pendell House.

William PELLATT (II) soon married again, in 1701, to Catherine GALE at Chichester. They had five further children in Pendell House: daughter Philippa, baptised 23 June 1702; twin sons Leonard and Henry, baptised 8 June 1704; and daughters Beckford, baptised 20 April 1708 and Catherine, baptised 18 August, 1710. Of the twins, Henry later became a clergyman and probably the donor to St Mary the Virgin Church, Blechingley, of a pewter plate, inscribed 'To W. Leonard Pellatt, died Aug 24 1752 aged 48'.

Regarding William (II) and Elizabeth's five children born in East Grinstead:

1. William (III) b. 1693 later married Margaret ? (who died 18 April 1777) and had two children, William (IV) b. 16 February 1728, bapt. 22 February and Thomas, b. 22 March 1729 and bapt. 28 March. His eldest son, William (IV), married Elizabeth PUPLET 29 June 1761, became a solicitor and died 19 June 1801. His wife Elizabeth had been buried at Blechingley 21 February 1797.

2. Edward married and had a daughter, Margaret, b. 19 December and bapt. 27 December 1723 but who, sadly, was buried 22 March the following year.

3 and 4. Elizabeth and Mary, died unmarried at Blechingley in 1759 and 1771.

5. Thomas, who was buried at Blechingley 14 January 1749, was known as 'Captain Pellatt', having joined the Royal Navy and been promoted to Lieutenant on 20 April 1727 and Commander on 29 July 1740. He was appointed Commanding Officer until June 1741 of HMS *Vulcan*, an 8-gun Fireship, and took part in operations against Cartagena, 3 April 1741 to May that year.

(A fireship, used in the days of wooden rowed or sailing ships, was a ship filled with combustibles, deliberately set on fire and steered (or, where possible, allowed to drift) into an enemy fleet, in order to destroy ships, or to create panic and make the enemy break formation.)

The Battle of Cartagena de Indias was an amphibious military engagement between the forces of Britain under Vice-Admiral Edward Vernon and those of Spain under Admiral Blas de Lezo. It took place at the city of Cartagena de Indias in 1741, in present-day Colombia. The battle was a significant episode of the large-scale naval campaign. It resulted in a major defeat for the British Navy and Army and caused heavy losses for the British. Disease (especially yellow fever), rather than deaths in combat, took the greatest toll among the British and Spanish forces.

1702

King William III died and Anne, aged 37, the second daughter of James II, became queen. It was during Anne's reign that the United Kingdom of Great Britain was created by the Union of England and Scotland.

She died in 1714 and although the throne would have gone to Sophia, James I's only daughter, she had died a few weeks before Anne, so the throne passed to her son, George.

1704

The Quitt Rents for the Manor of Blechingley record a sum of £1. 2s 6d to be paid by John GLYD Esq., 'for a Capital Messuage & Lands late in the occupation of Jn AMHERST Esq., now Mr Wm PELLATT'.

1705/6

William PELLATT is recorded as Churchwarden of Blechingley, and again in 1732.

1714

54-year-old George I, born in Hanover and son of Sophia and great-grandson of James I, arrived in England to become king, but was only able to speak a few words of English. National policy was therefore left to Sir Robert Walpole, who became Britain's first Prime Minister in 1721. The Jacobites (followers of James Stuart, son of James II) attempted to supplant George I in 1715 but failed.

1722

William PELLATT (II) died and was buried at Blechingley, 30 November. His son **William PELLAT**T (III) (1692–1751) thus inherited Pendell House and lived there with his wife Margaret and sons William (IV) (1728–1801) and Thomas.

1727

George I died during a visit to Hanover and was succeeded by his son, George II, who was the last English king to lead his army into battle (against the French at Dettingen in 1743).

1745

The Jacobites tried once again to place a Stuart on the throne and Prince Charles Edward Stuart (Bonnie Prince Charlie) landed in Scotland. He was routed at Culloden Moor in 1746 by the army under the Duke of Cumberland, known as 'Butcher' Cumberland. Prince Charles escaped to France and finally died a drunkard's death in Rome.

George II's reign was marked by the expansion of British influence in India under Robert Clive and Canada under James Wolfe.

THE JELFE FAMILY

1747

Andrews JELFE (1690–1759) purchased Pendell House from William PELLATT (III), who went to live at Croydon, where he died but was buried at Blechingley, 29 December 1751.

Andrews JELFE (his mother's maiden name was Andrews) was 'a mason who got considerably by his ingenuity in curing the defects of Westminster Bridge', which was completed by him in 1747. During his occupation of Pendell House he built the entrance courtyard, with its sedan chair gate and scalloped walls, as well as the well-proportioned scalloped wall with piers at the west end of the garden. The latter was built on a much older sunk brick wall, which had every appearance of being contemporary with the 1636 house.

At the age of 21, Andrews had married Elizabeth TURPIN, 17 April 1711, at St Mary the Virgin Church, Aldermanbury, London. He had been made free of the London Masons Company that year following his service with Edward STRONG, to whom he had been apprenticed in 1704. He was subsequently in partnership with Edward STRONG Junior and Christopher CASS, until December 1728 when STRONG withdrew.

Their son, also Andrews JELFE, had been baptised 21 September 1715 at St

Andrews JELFE.

Mary Mounthaw, London and another son, William, was born 11 June 1728 and baptised at Westminster, 27 June that year. Their daughter Elizabeth was baptised at St Mary at Lambeth on 14 September 1748.

Andrews JELFE had been appointed 'Architect and Clerk of the Works of all buildings erected or to be erected in the several garrisons, forts, castles, fortifications etc. belonging to the Office of Ordnance in Great Britain' in 1719. His first task was to begin the erection of barracks at Ruthven, Scotland, as well as to continue those at Killwhimen and Inversnaid already begun by his predecessor, James SMITH.

While in Scotland he was made a Burgess of Edinburgh. The following year he was transferred to Plymouth to supervise the construction of a new Gun Wharf or Ordnance Yard there. He also executed monumental sculpture, chimney pieces and other statuary work.

Andrews designed a house (not built) for a Mr Butler on Barn Hill, Stamford in 1731 and an ornamental alcove in 1753. The designs are preserved in the Bodleian Library. In 1733, Andrews put in one of the tenders for building apartments at the west end of the Bridewell Royal Hospital on the bank of the Thames. His offer of £4,300 was not accepted, the work going to Nathaniel EDMONDS for £3,950.

His biggest contract was the building of Westminster Bridge, to the design of Charles LABELYE. For this project he was in partnership with Samuel TUFNELL, the Master Mason to Westminster Abbey. The contract was signed 22 June 1738 and the bridge completed in 1747. JELFE had successfully overcome the structural problems caused by the sinking of the central pier by springing relieving arches across the spandrels of the adjacent arches.

By 1741 he had built 13 houses in two rows, adjoining the north side of New Palace Yard, London. His most important work as an architect was the Court House or Town Hall in Rye, Sussex in 1743.

The *Stanford Mercury* of 7 June 1744 had recorded that the Lord Mayor nominated Andrews JELFE Esq., Citizen and Mason, as a proper person for one of the Sheriffs of the City for the year ensuing. He declined this honour and was accordingly fined.

The 1746 *Westminster Rate Book* had recorded that Andrews JELFE was liable for sixteen shillings and seven pence for his property at New Palace Yard, St Margaret, Westminster.

1759

Andrews JELFE died 26 April and was buried 10 May that year at St Margaret, Westminster. His Will, made 5 March 1756, was an extremely long handwritten document, rambling in places, difficult to read and with countless repetitions of legal phrases.

It commenced with the instruction that he be:

> *buryed under of near the Sarcophagus of my Dear parents at South Weald with an additional inscription … of these words only 'Also Andrews their Son who Erected this and dyed in 17 ' and that it be carryed to the Grave by six poor house Labourers employed by my Nephew William Jelfe … the pall bearers to be six of my said Nephews to each of whom I order One Guinea, a two foot rule, a hatband and a pair of gloves.*

In essence, the Will gave his eldest son, Captain Andrews JELFE:

> *My mansion house at Pendhill in the parish of Blechingley, with the Outhouses, Gardens, Lands, Grounds and rudiaments and Appurtances, also the Terminal Lands adjoining thereto which I lately purchased of John Sonne Esquire, with the Appurtances and all my other messuages Lands Titles as will freehold as I hold within the said County of Surrey.*

He also gave Captain Andrews JELFE all his 13 freehold messuages or Tenements:

> *which I lately built and afterwards purchased of the Commissioners of the Sturminster Bridge … Situate in Two Rows adjoining together on the North side of Palace Yard and the South side of Bridge Street in the said parish of St Margaret, Sturminster.'*

He also gave his daughter, Elizabeth, the wife of Griffin RANSOM, Timber Merchant:

> *all my Stout Built Dwellinghouse Messuage or Tenement Situate on the East Side of Palace Yard aforesaid, now Occupyed by myself and*

90

said son Andrews with the Rooms over the gateway leading into my Working Yard … And I also Give and Devise unto my said Daughter the Stable and little Room adjoining to the Thames and behind my said house all the Range of Buildings Extending in a line East from my said house to the Thames and the Court on the other side my Working Yard adjoining to the Abutment of Westminster Bridge now also in the Occupation of myself and said son Andrews.

She was also given all his household goods and furniture, plate, and liquors, except money and securities for money, together with:

All that Messuages or Tenements Situate on the East Side of Palace Yard aforesaid and adjoining my said Working Yard together with my Wharf and Working Yard lying behind the said Messuage and the Counting House, Gateway and Appurtances to my said Yard and Wharf belonging all now in the possession of my said Nephew William Jelfe and also the little house adjoining thereto now or lately in the possession of Richard Tovey.

But there was provision for his nephew William JELFE to retain these premises to carry on the trade of a Mason for 21 years for a annual rent of £50 payable quarterly. Elizabeth also received the then very large sum of £10,000, on top of the £5,000 Bond he made when she married, also payable on his death.

He also gave his nephew, William JELFE, 'with whom I am now in partnership in Trade and as a reward for his Care and Diligence in carrying on my business I Give and Devise all Trade Implements and Working Tools made use of or belonging to my Business of a Mason'. William was also given 'the tenements in Holborn and in and near White Hart yard. together with the Messuage or tenement situate in North Street, Westminster, in the custody of my Cuze Thomas Caffer.'

£300 was given, to be equally divided among the children of his sister Mary, the same sum to be divided among the children of his late sister Margaret, also £300 to the children of his late sister Amelia and again £300 to the children of his late sister Elizabeth. His niece Jan MAYO received £200 and his niece Mary JELFE, sister of his nephew William JELFE, received £100.

John SMITH Esquire of Lambeth and his nephew William JELFE also received £20 apiece 'for mourning'. 'Good friends' Joseph CRANMER Esquire and Mr

Edmund HOLMES received 20 Guineas each and his son-in-law Griffin RANSOM had £500. The poor of the parish of South Weald were given £10 and the poor of the parish of Blechingley £5, distributed at the discretion of the Minister and Church Wardens, and all household servants who had been with him for a year received £5 'a piece for mourning'.

However, although he had earlier in his Will left £10,000 to his youngest son William JELFE, towards the end of the document he states:

> *whereas my said youngest Son William Jelfe has proved very idle*
> *and extravagant and I am in great fear he will wast the money*
> *herein Given and devised to him, Now out of Compassion to my said*
> *Son notwithstanding such his behaviour and to prevent his roming*
> *I Give and devise unto my said Son Andrews Jelfe the sum of five*
> *thousand pounds Upon Trust.*

The Will goes on to explain that his eldest son Andrews would only pay the interest to his brother William, on whose death the money would go to William's children, if any, otherwise shared between Andrews and his sister Elizabeth. It is quite clear from the Will that son Andrews and daughter Elizabeth were very much his favourites. Anything else in the estate not disposed of in the Will went to eldest son Andrews.

1759

Captain Andrews JELFE, (1715–1765) inherited Pendell House on the death of his father.

He was a Captain in the Royal Navy, and had married Elizabeth SMITH on 25 December 1745 at Southwark, St Mary Newington. Their daughter, Elizabeth, was baptised at Lambeth, 14 September 1748.

1760

George II died and was succeeded by his grandson, George III, who was the first English-born and English-speaking monarch since Queen Anne. His was the age of elegance, with such names as Jane Austen, Lord Byron, Shelley, Keats and Wordsworth. It was also the time of great statesmen like Pitt and Fox, and great military figures like General Wellington and Admiral Nelson.

1762 and 1763

Andrews JELFE is shown as a Qualified Freeholder and Copyholder for the Tandridge Hundred.

1763

Amelia JELFE, daughter of Captain Andrews and Elizabeth JELFE, was baptised at St Mary, Lambeth, Surrey.

1764

Andrews Smith JELFE, son of Captain Andrews JELFE and his wife Elizabeth, was baptised 8 September 1764 in Blechingley.

1765

Captain Andrews JELFE died on 15 March and was buried at St Mary Church, Lambeth, Surrey. His probate records states:

> *memo. That Andrews Jelfe of Pendhill in Surrey Esq. died possessed of Five thousand pounds Consolidated four per cent Annuities and dying Intestate Letters of Administration dated at Doctors Commons June 1ˢᵗ 1765 were granted to Elizabeth Jelfe now his Widow by relief who may dispose of the said £5,000. Registered June 14 1765.*
>
> *S. Bretland.*

1766

Three years earlier, in 1763, there was a great epidemic in London, when deaths from small-pox numbered 3,582. It came to Blechingley in 1766 when Mr J. G. PERKINS, writing to his brother-in-law, said 'Miss Hall has been dead about six weeks and Charles Best died about a week ago of the small-pox in the Pest House. There are about 18 in the Pest House now.'

1768

On 26 September, Griff RANSOM, Andrews' brother-in-law, certified that there was:

> *£26,500 Stock in three & a half percent Annuities standing in the joint names of John Smith of Lambeth; Thomas Ransom of Ipswich*

in Suffolk and Andrews Jelfe of Pendhill in Surrey and that since the Acceptance of Said Stock Andrews Jelfe Esq deceased as Appears by Letters of Administration (he dying Intestate) which were granted at Doctors Commons the 1ˢᵗ day of June 1765 unto Elizabet Jelfe his Widow & Relief wherein he is dismembered of Blechingley in the County of Surrey therefore the above Stock remains at the disposal of the above John Smith and Thomas Ransom. Registered 26ᵗʰ September 1768 John Rogers. N.1028.

1773
The 'Boston Tea Party' was the first sign of troubles that were to come in the American colony.

1776
Following the American War of Independence, the American Colonies proclaimed their independence on 4 July. George III suffered from a mental illness due to intermittent porphyria, and eventually became blind and insane.

1779
On 25 July, a subscription was raised for placing eight new bells, together with a new bell frame, stocks and wheels, in Blechingley parish church. Among the contributors were 'John Kenrick Esq., Member of Parliament for this Boro, £44, 3s 6; The Revd. Dr. Kenrick, Rector and Brother to this Member, £25; Mrs Jelfe of Pendhill House, £25'.

1783
October – Act of Parliament for raising a tax of threepence on the registering of all births, marriages and burials.

1784
The *Reading Mercury* on 13 December reported the marriage of George Mackett Esq of Southampton to Miss JELFE, eldest daughter of the late Andrews JELFE Esq of Pendhill in Surrey.

1791
The first bicycle, called a Velocipede, was built by the French nobleman Comte de Sivrac. It had two wheels, a saddle and was foot powered.

1793

The *Derby Mercury* of 12 November carried an advertisement giving the full details of the 'neat household furniture' to be sold by auction, belonging to Joseph Seymour BISCOE Esq. of Edge Hill, near Duffield, Derby.

1798

Joseph Seymour BISCOE is recorded as a Churchwarden of Blechingley.

1802

Morning Post, 2 April – 'Died at Brompton in her 72nd year, Mrs JELFE, releci of Captain Andrews JELFE, late of Pendhill, Surrey.'

Andrews Smith JELFE, son of Captain Andrews and Elizabeth JELFE and living in Pimlico, was buried 17 June at St Mary, Lambeth, Surrey,

Humphry Davy invented the first electric light. He experimented with electricity and invented an electric battery. When he connected wires to his battery and a piece of carbon, the carbon glowed, producing light. His invention was known as the Electric Arc lamp. While it produced light, it didn't produce it for long and was much too bright for practical use.

THE BISCOE FAMILY

1803

Joseph Seymour BISCOE, 42 years (1761–1835) married to Stephana née Law, 27 years, (1776–1849) purchased Pendell House. He was said to have a great interest in antiquarian matters and had suggested that the builder of Pendell Court descended from Sir John HOLMAN, standard-bearer to Sir William RUSSELL at Bosworth Field.

(The Battle of Bosworth Field was the last significant battle of the Wars of the Roses, the civil war between the Houses of Lancaster and York.)

The couple had married on 12 February 1799 and their children were born in Pendell House – Louisa Mary in 1804; William in 1805; Ann Jane in 1807 and Joseph in 1808. It was Joseph's second marriage, his first was to Susanna Harriet HOPE, 18 years (1768–1839), daughter of the Rev. Charles HOPE, Rector of All Saints, Derby, on 22 May 1786, with whom he had a daughter, Mary, in 1787 in Boughton, Northamptonshire.

Mary was later married by the Right Rev. the Lord Bishop of Gloucester to Sir Robert INGLIS, 10 February 1807, in St Marylebone and died 12 October 1872, aged 85, in Bloomsbury, Middlesex. She was buried in the INGLIS family vault, which was then sealed as she was the last member of the family. Sir Robert was the MP for Oxford University and died at his home, 7 Redford Square, London, 5 May 1855. As they had no children, the baronetcy became extinct.

Joseph's fifth daughter, Frances Agnata, married George BASEVI Esq. of Saville Row, London, on 30 March 1830 at Cheltenham. Another daughter, Caroline Octavia, died 30 January 1908, aged 88, at Playford Mount, Suffolk. She was the widow, first, of Sir William STEVENSON, K.C.B., Governor of Mauritius, and secondly of the Rev. F. Barham ZINCKE, Vicar of Wherstead and Chaplain-in-Ordinary to the Queen.

The reason for Joseph's second marriage was because on 8 December 1794, Susanna BISCOE went on trial with a special jury before Lord Chief Justice KENYON for adultery with Robert GORDON. The case was fully reported in the *Ross-shire Journal* on 4 October 1907 because it was considered to have involved important barristers, including the Hon. Thomas Erskine.

The facts of the case were that Joseph was 25 years old when first married, his wife only 18, and in May 1794 they rented Shorum House, Kent, owned by Robert GORDON, a former school friend of Joseph. Robert was a wealthy man, owning a large estate in the West Indies, giving an income of £4,000 to £5,000 a year, as well as property in Scotland.

He lived just six miles from Shorum House, which he visited frequently. It was during these visits that the servants, who gave evidence, suspected that he and Mrs BISCOE were 'having an improper relationship'. However, none of the servants thought it their place to mention it to Joseph BISCOE.

Evidence was given of Robert GORDON and Mrs BISCOE being left alone until the early hours whilst her husband, Joseph, went to bed by 10 or 11 o'clock, also of the couple being in the house on their own whilst Joseph went shooting on the estate. The defence tried to persuade the jury that Joseph had, in effect, turned a blind eye to the relationship growing between GORDON and Mrs BISCOE, but Robert GORDON, through his counsel, admitted adultery, thus avoiding details of their affair being given. GORDON was described during the trial as 'a stout, healthy young man'.

Matters had come to a head on 21 October 1794, when Joseph BISCOE was in London on business, when the servants saw Mrs BISCOE and Robert

GORDON leave the house together in a post-chaise. The BISCOE coachman followed and caught them up, but could not persuade the couple to return, and they continued to GORDON's house, where they remained living together, hence the court proceedings. Joseph BISCOE had asked for £10,000 damages but the jury, who had retired for a short time, awarded him £5,000 (a still not inconsiderable sum!) and a divorce soon followed.

Joseph Seymour BISCOE was the only son of Vincent John BISCOE, described as a West India Merchant of London (1721–1770) and Lady Mary SEYMOUR (1729–1762). (His mother was the only daughter of Edward, 8th Duke of Somerset.) He attended Trinity College, Cambridge at the age of 17, having matriculated from Harrow School, and gained an MA.

He was admitted to Lincoln's Inn on 19 November 1781, one of the four Inns of Court in London to which barristers of England and Wales belong and where they are called to the Bar. It is recognised to be one of the world's most prestigious professional bodies of judges and lawyers and is the largest Inn.

It is believed to be named after Henry de Lacy, 3rd Earl of Lincoln. The Inn is also well known for its large garden and library, which have existed since 1422.

Joseph was an active magistrate and Lambert's *Blechingley Parish History* states 'his beautifully neat hand appears often in parish documents' and he supplied a good deal of material to Manning's great *Surrey County History*.

1809

Sir William BENSLEY, who married Mary (1759–), Joseph Seymour BISCOE's sister, died and his monument is in the north-east corner of the Ham Chapel in the Church of St Mary the Virgin, Blechingley. The monument, with its ship and elephant, by John BACON Jnr, is considered to be a fine example of sculpture.

The full wording on the monument is given in Appendix 'A'.

THE PERKINS FAMILY

1811

George IV ruled as Prince Regent after 1811 until his father's death in 1820.

John G. W. PERKINS, a wealthy man and member of the Stock Exchange, bought Pendell House, in trust for his son John, from Joseph BISCOE, who moved to Hempstead, Gloucestershire and died in Clifton, Gloucestershire, 5 May 1835 at the age of 74. His widow, Stephana BISCOE, died at Bath, 28 February 1849.

John G. W. PERKINS bought a good deal of land in Blechingley, including all of nearby Town Farm and had inherited Pendell Court from his half-sister, Mrs Hester Wade SCULLARD when she died in 1799.

Mr J. G. W. PERKINS and his wife Margaret. (Courtesy of Dame Sarah GOAD.)

The SCULLARDS and PERKINS families had lived at Pendell Court together for many years and were inter-related. John G. W.'s father, also John, had married Annabella SEYLIARD, Mrs SCULLARD's paternal aunt, as his first wife.

His second wife was her widowed mother, Margaret SEYLIARD, a great-niece of Jeffrey AMHERST, the MP of 1689.

1813

In the summer of 1813, some of Mr PERKINS' workmen, 'in grubbing up the bank of a hedge in a level field, a little distance N.E. of his house, Pendell Court, struck on a stone wall. By his direction they traced it and found the foundation of a room, which appears to have been a hypocaust at a small distance under the surface of a field. This room was nearly filled with broken tiles of Roman workmanship.' The account goes on to what clearly were the remains of a Roman building, which Mr PERKINS covered with a thatched roof.

1820

George III died at Windsor Castle and his son, the Prince Regent, became George IV. George IV led an extravagant lifestyle that contributed to the fashions of the Regency era. He was a patron of new forms of leisure, style and taste and commissioned John Nash to build the Royal Pavilion in Brighton and remodel Buckingham Palace, and Sir Jeffry Wyattville to rebuild Windsor Castle.

1827 John G. W. PERKINS died and was succeeded by his son John, who thus became the owner of Pendell Court.

1829

The two MPs for Blechingley, (originally with only 46 voters, therefore called a 'Rotten Borough') were William LAMB, who became Lord MELBOURNE, Prime Minister 1834–41, mentor of the young Queen Victoria, and Lord PALMERSTON, who voted for the 1832 Reform Bill which removed the 'Rotten Borough of Blechingley', so it no longer had an MP.

1830

George IV died at Windsor Castle and his only legitimate child, Princess Charlotte of Wales, had died from post-partum complications in 1817, after delivering a stillborn son. The second son of George III, Prince Frederick, Duke of York and Albany, had died childless in 1827, so the succession passed to George IV's brother, the third son of George III, Prince William, Duke of Clarence, who reigned as William IV. As Prince William, he had served in the Royal Navy for 10 years and was thus known as 'The Sailor King'.

Almshouses were built by Clara Matilda PERKINS, the Lady of the Manor, on the site of the Old Hall House. (They were sold to Godstone R.D.C. who built new old people's dwellings on the site in 1965.)

1834

When slavery was abolished in 1834, compensation was awarded by the Government, no, not to the unfortunate slaves but to their wealthy 'owners'. It beggars belief that the often inhumane treatment to the innocent victims was rewarded when their free services were no longer available, but that was the way of the world at that time. (The total of 238 individuals in Surrey who 'owned' slaves are recorded in 'Legacies of British Slave-ownership', accessed on the website www.ucl.ac.uk/lbs/search.)

One of the slave 'owners' was John PERKINS' immediate neighbour, CHARLES JOHN MANNING of Pendell Court. He was an absentee landlord, as Trustee, of the Lower Walrond & Upper Walrond Estates in Antigua which had 233 slaves. For this he was awarded £3,626 12s 1d, a massive sum for this period. He also owned another estate in Antigua, Little Duers, with 73 slaves, for which he would have received £889 10s 1d, but for some unknown reason his application was unsuccessful.

Charles MANNING was a West India merchant, the son of William Manning (1777–1835) and Mary Hunter (1771–1847), and a co-trustee (with the Earl of Rosslyn) under the marriage settlement of Bethell Walrond and Lady Janet St Claire. It was for this reason that he was awarded compensation for the Upper and Lower Walrond estates in Antigua.

His father William Manning was a West India merchant and landowner in St Kitts, MP for Lymington 1801–1806, Evesham 1806–1818 and Penryn 1826--830, and a leading voice in the West India lobby.

Charles died on 29 November 1880 at 15 Princes Gardens, Knightsbridge, Middlesex, aged 81, leaving effects under £70,000. He was brother of Henry Edward Manning (1808–1892), Roman Catholic convert and Archbishop of Westminster (1865–1892) and Cardinal (1875–1892).

1835

John G. PERKINS Jnr, the owner of Pendell Court, inherited Pendell House from his father, John G. W. PERKINS. On 15 September that year the greater part of Blechingley, together with the Manor, were put up for auction by the trustees, under Acts of Parliament. Particulars of the sale were held by Messrs. Blake of Croydon at the White Hart Inn, Blechingley, and John PERKINS Esq. of Pendell Court acquired the manor for the princely sum of £540.

1837

William IV died at Windsor Castle, where he was buried, and the throne was inherited by Princess Victoria, the only child of Edward, Duke of Kent, the fourth son of George III.

1840

Queen Victoria married her cousin, Albert of Saxe-Coburg, who exerted tremendous influence over the queen. He left two legacies, the Christmas tree and the Great Exhibition of 1851. Money from the exhibition helped to create the Victoria & Albert Museum, the Science Museum, Imperial College and the Royal Albert Hall. Queen Victoria's reign saw the British Empire double in size.

1841 Census

The Census Returns of 1841 to 1871 are somewhat confusing, as Pendell and Pendhill are shown intermittently, as well as two Pendhills. It is consistently Pendell from 1881 onwards. It would also appear that of the two properties known as just Pendhill, either side of Lake Cottage, one was actually Pendell House, occupied mainly by the **KENRICK** family.

It also appears that the four cottages at the rear of Pendell House are also included as part of the house, whether shown as Pendhill or Pendell. They were used as stables, stores and living accommodation for servants. Lake Cottage, sometimes mentioned, was in the most southern section of the grounds.

In 1841, one 'Pendhill' had a large number of occupants, including the Sarah SEAWELL family, and Pendell Court occupied by John PERKINS. It was followed by another 'Pendhill' occupied by Mary KENRICK, 63, Independent, Caroline, 30, also Independent and William KENRICK, 30, Barrister. They had two female servants. It thus appears that although John PERKINS owned Pendell House, he allowed members of the **KENRICK** family, to whom he was related, to live there.

The Tithe Map of 1841 showed that Mr John PERKINS owned Pendell Court with over 650 acres adjoining, including 'Stichens' with its cottages, as well as other properties. It was said he was 'thus, after Sir William CLAYTON, by far the largest landowner in the parish, but as he died unmarried and intestate in 1846 his estate was divided up between his four surviving sisters'.

1846

The Railway Company Rates were assessed at £1,937. 10s, paying £24. 4s 4d on a 3d Rate. Mr PERKINS, the next highest, at £533. 15s paying £6. 13s 5d, a long way above the next highest.

Margaret (Maria) TROTTER (1796–1861) sister of John Perkins Jnr., inherited Pendell House on his death. She is shown as 45 years old on the 1841 census, living in Horton Place, Epsom, with husband John Trotter, 60 years, of

Independent Means. The 1861 Census shows her at the same address, but now a widow. Although Mrs TROTTER owned Pendell House she, like her brother, clearly allowed members of the family, PERKINS and **KENRICK**, who would eventually own it, to live there.

THE KENRICK FAMILY

The KENRICK crest. Ermine, a lion rampant sable. Motto 'Vertue is Honour'. (Courtesy of Dame Sarah GOAD.)

Blechingley – A Parish History states:

> *'The name of PERKINS disappeared with the purchase of Pendell Court by Sir George MacLEAY and the oldest residential name left in the parish was that of KENRICK, which first appeared in Blechingley when the Rev. Matthew KENRICK became rector in 1775.'*

Rev. Matthew KENRICK, a relative of the CLAYTON family, was Rector from 1775 until he died in 1803 and he supervised the building of the Churchyard retaining wall in Church Lane in 1778. He also installed a new peal of bells in 1780.

Rev. Matthew KENRICK (1736–1803). (Courtesy of Dame Sarah GOAD.)

John KENRICK MP. (1735–1799)

Rev. Jarvis KENRICK, Rector 1803–1838. (Courtesy of Dame Sarah GOAD.)

John KENRICK had sat for Blechingley in the two Parliaments of 1780 and 1784, but he died only four months after possessing the Manor and devised both Manor and Borough to his brother, the Rev. Matthew KENRICK, LL.D., then Rector of Blechingley. Dr KENRICK, who never married, survived only four years and left it to a third brother, the Rev. Jarvis KENRICK, who was Vicar of Chilham in Kent for 50 years and died in 1809. His son, also the Rev. Jarvis KENRICK, had already succeeded his uncle, Dr KENRICK, as Rector of Blechingley in 1803 and became Lord of the Manor also in 1809.

William KENRICK, Esq., of Blechingley and of Middle Temple was re-elected as MP for 1806–1807 on his appointment as Master of the Household.

He had sold both Manor and Borough in 1816 to Matthew RUSSELL Esq., of Portland Place, London, for the sum of £6,000. The Reform Bill in 1832 swept away both Blechingley seats, but for the last year of its existence as a Borough, Blechingley had for one of its members a man who became perhaps the most famous statesman ever connected with it, Viscount PALMERSTON.

Blechingley – A Parish History states: 'It was to the generosity of Mrs Kenrick, widow of the Rev. Jarvis Kenrick, rector of Blechingley, and her two sisters, Mrs Trotter and Miss Perkins, sisters and co-heiresses of Mr John Perkins Jnr. of Pendell Court, that the parish owed the building of the north aisle' (i.e. of St Mary the Virgin Church, Blechingley).

The CLAYTON family, one of the most important families in the village, borne out by the imposing monument of Sir Robert and Martha CLAYTON inside St Mary the Virgin Church, Blechingley, have a close relationship with the KENRICK family. It is shown by an entry in *Blechingley, A Parish History* that states: 'Sir Kenrick Clayton had, by deed dated May 30th 1745, granted the next presentation to his first cousin and brother-in-law Mr Matthew Kenrick, sixth son of John Kenrick of Flore or Flower in Godstone, whose wife was a daughter Alderman Perient Trott and sister of Sir Robert Clayton's wife, the lady of the great Blechingley monument.'

1851 Census

This shows Mary, Caroline and William KENRICK, Clara PERKINS and eight staff living in Pendell, which must be Pendell House as the 1855 *Kelly's Street Directory* shows Pendell House occupied by Mrs Mary KENRICK and Miss Clara Margaret PERKINS. The other Pendhill (possibly one of the cottages) still contains Sarah SEAWELL as Head.

Mrs Mary KENRICK was the daughter of John G. W. PERKINS of Pendell Court and had married the Rev. Jarvis KENRICK, then aged 28, 16 April 1804. They were the grandparents of the Jarvis KENRICK who inherited Pendell House in 1887.

1856

The North Aisle of St Mary the Virgin Church, Blechingley, was a gift from Mrs KENRICK, widow of the late Rector.

1861

Maria TROTTER died 27 December, at her home Horton Place, Epsom, and her Will showed she had personal effects valued under £20,000. It was proved by Maria KENRICK, spinster, of Pendell, near Blechingley.

So Pendell House passed to Maria TROTTER's nieces, **Caroline KENRICK (1808–1887) and Clara Matilda Charles KENRICK (1809–1880)**.

The Street Directory also includes: 'The Church of St Mary the Virgin is a large building. The living is a Rectory and held by the Rev. Chas. Fox CHAWNER, M.A. Here is a Charity School supported by Misses Kenrick and a Free Grammar Sch. for 25 boys. There are 4 Alms Houses for widows, erected by Miss C.M. PERKINS.'

The 1861 Census

This repeats the same pattern as the 1851 Census, but with the two Pendhills following one another directly, one with Sarah SEAWELL, 66, Fundholder as Head, with three servants and the other with Caroline KENRICK, 52, Landed Gentlewoman, Proprietor & Fundholder as Head. Her two sisters, Clara, 51, and Maria, 47, are shown with the same titles as Caroline.

They had eight servants, a Parlour Maid, two Lady's Maids, Cook, Housemaid, Assistant Housemaid, Gardener and Footman. Clara M. C. PERKINS, aunt to the KENRICK sisters, was also present, aged 69 and a Fund holder. (It should be noted that all the KENRICK females and servants were unmarried.)

1867 Kelly's Street Directory

This confirms that Pendell House was occupied by Misses Caroline & Clara KENRICK and Miss PERKINS.

1870

Clara Matilda Charles *(sic)* PERKINS, spinster, died 11 May at Pendell Court with personal effects valued under £25,000 and her Will was proved by the Rev. Jarvis KENRICK of Caterham, nephew.

1871 Census

This time the KENRICK family, Clara, 61, Maria, 57, with nieces Fanny KENRICK, 24 and Etheldred KENRICK, 22 and six servants are shown in Pendell House, between Lake Cottages and Pendell Court, whilst this time Sarah SEAWELL is also shown in Pendhill House.

It would thus seem that Sarah SEAWELL, 76, Annuitant, was living in one of the four cottages at the rear of Pendell House.  She had five servants, a Housekeeper, Cook, Housemaid, Gardener, and General Servant.

The situation is again confirmed in the 1874 *Kelly's Street Directory* where the Misses KENRICK are shown in Pendell House.

This early 13th-century font, built in the reign of King John and from the parish church of St Lawrence, Caterham, was presented to St John the Evangelist's Church, Caterham Valley, by the Rector, Revd. Jarvis KENRICK in 1871. It was restored in his memory by his widow in 1881.

1876

Queen Victoria became Empress of India. Alexander Graham BELL made the first telephone call, on 10 March.

1878

Thomas Edison began serious research into developing a practical incandescent lamp and on 14 October 1878, Edison filed his first patent application for 'Improvement In Electric Lights'.

1880

Clara KENRICK died 7 April at Pendell House, with a personal estate valued at under £14,000. Her nephew, Jarvis KENRICK, proved the Will. St Mary the Virgin Church, Blechingley, has, under a beautiful stained glass window, 'In memory of Clara Kenrick who died April 7, 1880'. Owing to the objections of one of the then churchwardens, this window was not put up until after the death of the two Misses KENRICK, who had given it in memory of their sister.

Edison and his team discovered that a carbonised bamboo filament could last over 1,200 hours. This discovery marked the beginning of commercially manufactured light bulbs and in 1880 Thomas Edison's company, Edison Electric Light Company, began marketing its new product.

1881 Census

Caroline and Maria KENRICK are still in Pendell House, with a Cook, Housemaid, Under Housemaid, Parlour Maid and Groom, whilst a Coachman, his wife and Gardener and his wife are living in Pendell (almost certainly in the row of cottages behind Pendell House).

The Savoy Theatre was the first building to be fitted with electric light bulbs.

1882

The Street Directories show Miss KENRICK in Pendell, the 'late Miss C. M. PERKINS' in Pendell House in 1887 and the Misses KENRICK in Pendell House in 1890.

1884

Jarvis KENRICK (1852–1949) married Lillian Helen JAFFREY (and had nine daughters).

1885

The first car, with a petrol powered internal combustion engine, was built by Karl BENZ in Mannheim, Germany.

1887

Jarvis KENRICK (1852–1949) inherited Pendell House on the death of his aunt, Caroline KENRICK, who died 29 December with a personal estate valued at £12,788. 2s 9d.

St Mary the Virgin Church, Blechingley, has a white marble sarcophagus, on a grey background surmounted by an urn, dedicated to his grandfather. It states:

> *Sacred to the Memory of The Revd. Jarvis Kenrick, 35 years rector of this parish, who died the 21ˢᵗ of November 1838 in the 64ᵗʰ year of his age. And of Mary, widow of the above who died 31ˢᵗ May 1859, aged 81 years. Also to Frances, youngest daughter of Jarvis and Mary Kenrick, who died the 24ᵗʰ August 1834 in the 20ᵗʰ year of her age.*

(This Mrs Mary KENRICK was one of the four daughters of Mr J. G. W. PERKINS of Pendell Court.)

1891 Census

This records only Maria KENRICK, 77, with four Domestic Servants, Ladies Maid and Groom in Pendell House. Jarvis, however, is shown as living in 'Colley Stables', Colley, Reigate, with his wife Lillian and five daughters plus seven servants.

1893

William Abraham BELL purchased Pendell Court. It is said that he was on holiday in France when he met Uvedale LAMBERT who told him of the availability of the finest and most important mansion in the Parish.

1895

The Street Directory shows that Miss KENRICK was in Pendell.

Jarvis KENRICK wrote to the *Surrey Mirror* on 23 August that year, complaining about the lack of a full-time sanitary inspector for Reigate. A Mr Thomas STEEL replied in the paper on 25 August, attacking Jarvis for complaining, saying, 'I have known Mr Jarvis for a number of years, as being engaged in various matters, but his success has not been great in anything. His attempts to gain a seat on the Council or Board of Guardians have always failed.'

An article in the *Dorking & Leatherhead Advertiser* on 11 November 1899 mentioned that Mr Jarvis KENRICK of Pendell, Blechingley, had succeeded Captain POLLEN, R.N., in the Hon. Secretaryship of the Reigate Division of the Soldiers and Sailors' Family Association. The paper also printed a letter from Jarvis in which he appealed for funds.

1901

Queen Victoria died and Edward VII came to the throne. Thus started what was called 'The Edwardian Age'. Edward had married the beautiful Alexandra of Denmark in 1863 and they had six children. Edward VII's best known mistress was Lillie Langtry, known as 'Jersey Lily'.

1901 Census for Pendell House

This shows Jarvis, Retired Solicitor and Lillian Helen KENRICK as occupiers, **with nine daughters** and a Governess, Cook, Parlour Maid, three Housemaids, two Children's Maids, Kitchen Maid, two Laundry Maids and a Groom.

Jarvis KENRICK. (Courtesy of Dame Sarah GOAD.)

'Pendell Stables' is shown for the first time, with a Groom, and his wife resident with their six children. Shown in a 'Room over Stables' were two Gardeners, and a Coachman with his wife and daughter.

It is of interest to know that Jarvis scored the first ever goal in an FA Cup Final, aged only 19, in 1871. He netted the opening goal in a 3–0 victory for Clapham Rovers at Upton Park, scoring two goals in total. He subsequently was in the winning team winning the FA Cup for three years running with the Wanderers. He scored in two consecutive cup finals, in 1877 and again the following year, when he scored twice.

He also made a first-class appearance for Surrey County Cricket Club in 1876, as a right-hand bat and left-arm medium bowler and was the Secretary of the Croquet Association from 1904 to 1909.

Jarvis was also a keen photographer, contributing most of the photo illustrations in Uvedale Lambert's two-volume history of Blechingley in 1921.

Born in Chichester, 13 November 1852, he was the son of Jarvis KENRICK (1805–1879), the Rector of Caterham (whose father was also Jarvis KENRICK!) and was the last KENRICK to live in Blechingley. He died in Sussex on 29 January 1949, aged 97.

109

The former Caterham Rectory.

The family lived in Caterham from 1841–1915, and in 2013 a plaque was unveiled at their former Rectory, now Cedar House, in the High Street, the home of Buxton Construction.

A lovely Victorian group at the front of Pendell House. (Courtesy of Derek MOORE.)
It is extremely likely that this was taken c.1905, showing the KENRICK family. It is thought that the nine daughters are shown with their mother. If so they are Mary, 19yrs; Helen, 18yrs; Dorothy, 17yrs; Ethelared, 15yrs; Margaret, 14yrs; Ruth, 12yrs; Alison, 12yrs; Joyce, 10yrs and Evelyn, 8yrs with Mrs Lillian Helen JARVIS, 43yrs.

1903

On 17 December, Orville and Wilbur WRIGHT made the first successful flight in a self-propelled heavier-than-air aircraft near Kitty Hawk, North Carolina.

1903–1915 Kelly's Street Directories

These show Jarvis KENRICK as the occupier of Pendell House.

1909

Jarvis KENRICK, Esq., is recorded as a Churchwarden of Blechingley until 1914.

1910

George V came to the throne on the death of his father, Edward VII. George had joined the Royal Navy as a cadet in 1877 and loved the sea.

1911 Census for Pendell House

This showed Jarvis KENRICK, 58, Retired Solicitor, with his wife Lillian Helen, seven daughters and seven servants, Governess, Cook, Parlour Maid, Kitchen Maid, Housemaid, Sewing Maid, and Under Housemaid in the house. The 'Pendell House Laundry' is also shown (assumed to be one of the four cottages) with a Handyman & Gardener with his wife and two children, together with a Laundress.

1914

World War One broke out on 4 August.

1915

Jarvis KENRICK is recorded on 8 October as a passenger on board the 2,342-ton SS *Serrana* departing from London bound for Demerara in British Guyana, in the West Indies. The ship was carrying eight adults and four children. Jarvis was the only Englishman on board, travelling alone, and was making a round trip, returning to London. The other passengers were disembarking at Trinidad, Demerara and Barbados.

He was then 63, so it would seem he was now retired and had placed his home up for sale, subsequently occupied by **Charles Egerton MOTT** and his family in 1916.

THE MOTT FAMILY

Some unexpected MOTT family information was revealed in the BBC1 television programme *Who Do You Think You Are?*, broadcast at 8 p.m. on 8 March 2017. Sophie RAWORTH, a television presenter, was the subject and her Great-Grandmother was Amy MOTT, daughter of Henry Isaac MOTT. The programme was of interest to the author as he knew that the MOTT family had owned Pendell House from 1916 to 1936.

The programme revealed that members of the MOTT family, in the Regency period, were renowned Grand Piano makers, with premises at 92, Pall Mall, London, and a Grand Piano made by I. H. R. MOTT and J. C. MOTT was in the Brighton Pavilion in 1820, made for George IV. The makers were Isaac Henry MOTT (**not** Sophie RAWORTH's Henry Isaac) and Julius Caesar MOTT, neither being directly related to Sophie but certainly related to the MOTT family who later purchased Pendell House. (Julius was the grandfather of Charles Egerton MOTT who lived there from 1916.)

The MOTT family originated in Birmingham, where William MOTT's son Julius Caesar and his brother Isaac Robert MOTT's son, Isaac Henry Robert MOTT, were both recorded as Pianoforte Makers in London (as stated on the Brighton Pavilion Grand Piano). William had married Martha BARROWCLIFFE on 2 August 1779 in Birmingham, where his son Samuel was born in 1784 and son Julius Caesar born 7 November 1788. (It was Samuel's son Henry Isaac, born 1815, who was the ancestor of Sophie RAWORTH. Samuel moved to Jersey, where he committed suicide in 1838.)

What was especially interesting was that in 1790, William MOTT, recorded as a Plated Buckley *(form of jewellery)* Maker, and his wife Martha, were living in Fleet Street, Birmingham. The following year there were riots in Birmingham, lasting three days and nights, directed against Dissenter Churches, i.e. Protestant churches that did not recognise the King as head of the Church and were seen as a threat to the State. Dissenters, such as Baptist and Methodists, were deprived of many rights unless they abandoned their church. One such church was the New Jerusalem Church in Fleet Street, Birmingham, where William and Martha MOTT lived and were also members.

In spite of the 1791 riots, when 27 dissenter homes were destroyed, the five MOTT children were all baptised in the New Jerusalem Church on 15 April 1792. The children were William, b.16 June 1781; Samuel, b. 28 May 1784;

Jemima, b. 10 April 1786; Julius b. 7 November 1788, and Martha, b. 23 July 1791. (Julius Caesar's official baptism record states it was the 'New Jerusalemite Swedenborgian' denomination.)

It can thus be seen that although strong-willed Martha was heavily pregnant with her daughter Martha during the riots, she nevertheless went ahead with the baptisms the following year in spite of the threats. A further daughter, Mary Ann, was baptised on 19 May 1793.

Because of the continued antagonism against dissenters and following Mary Ann's baptism, the family moved to New York, USA, in 1793, living at 240 Water Street at the southern tip of Manhattan. The New Jerusalem Church in Fleet Street, Birmingham, had been fire-bombed by then. Together with the BRAGG family, who had also moved from Birmingham and were members of the New Jerusalem Church, they almost immediately, after holding meetings in the BRAGGs' house, formed a fresh New Jerusalem Church. They were taking advantage of the religious freedom they found there.

However, sadly, yellow fever spread throughout the district, brought in by mosquitoes on board ships calling there, and it claimed the lives of Mrs BRAGG and three of her children, as well as William and Martha MOTT. William Barrowcliffe MOTT and six of the orphaned MOTT children were then returned to England with friends, including Julius Caesar MOTT, who went on to marry Eliza THOMPSON on 20 September 1816 at St Leonard, Shoreditch. They had a daughter, Eliza MOTT b. 23 February 1819 and three sons, Albert Julius MOTT b. 1 October 1821, Henry Fearson MOTT b. 19 March 1829 and **Charles Grey MOTT** b. 27 May 1833.

Charles Grey MOTT (1833–1905), the father of **Charles Egerton MOTT** (1871–1931) who occupied Pendell House in 1916, first warrants some mention.

Charles Grey MOTT was born in Loughborough, Leicestershire, the son of the quaintly named Julius Caesar MOTT, who had died in 1859, and his wife Eliza THOMPSON. Charles married Sophie THORNELY in early 1857 and they had six children, Eliza, b. 1859 (who died unmarried in 1885); Constance, b. 1860; Mary Cresswell, b. 1862; Samuel Thornely, b. 1864; Clara Isabella, b. 1867; and Charles Egerton, b. 1871.

The family lived in Cheshire until 1891, when they moved to Middlesex, and he was shown on various census forms as 1861 – Coal Merchant employing 9 men; 1871 – Coal Merchant; 1881 – Colliery Proprietor and Railway Director; 1891 and 1901 – Magistrate & Railway Director.

Records show he was a Director of the following: The Great Western Railway (of which he was also Chairman); Kirkcaldy & District Railway Company; Scarborough, Bridlington and West Riding Railway Company; Mersey Railway Company; Burley, Clitheroe and Sabden Railway Company; Midland Uruguay Railway and the City and South London Railway Company (of which he was also Chairman).

He was also a Director of the Peruvian Corporation in Peru, which owned the revenue from 769 miles of the State Railway, an annual sum of over £120,000. It also had the right to all Guano discovered, up to 2,000,000 tons and the concession for a railway to the navigable waters of the Amazon.

It also owned the Cerro de Pasco Silver Mines, having a gross average of £400,000 'even when worked in a primitive manner without modern machinery and believed to be inexhaustible'.

On 22 November 1884, the *Cheshire Observer* reported the voluntary winding up of the Neston Colliery Co. Ltd.

It was registered 16 September 1874:

> *the objects for which it was established being to purchase from*
> *Mr Charles Grey Mott of Birkenhead, for £48,000 payable £18,000*
> *in cash and £80,000 in fully paid-up shares in the capital of the*
> *company, all his rights and interest in a certain agreement made*
> *between the Most Noble Henry, Duke of Norfolk and the Right*
> *Honourable Edward George, Baron Howard of Glossop, of the one*
> *part, and Charles Grey Mott of the other, and also 20 acres of freehold*
> *land in the parish of Neston, in the county of Chester, and Mr Mott's*

interests in sundry other memoranda respecting land, coal, clay and ironstone within the manor of Little Neston, the capital being £100,000 in 10,000 shares of £10 each. Mr Mott received his 3,000 shares and subscribed himself for 850 others, so the cash he received was about £10,000 only.

Charles Grey MOTT died in Hendon 7 November 1905 and his Will that year showed he possessed £23,652. 8s 9d, a not inconsiderable sum at that time. His funeral was reported in the *London Daily News* on 11 November 1905, headed 'Railway Director's Funeral'. It stated:

Mr Charles Grey Mott of Harrow Weald Lodge, Chairman of the City and South London Railway and the 'father' of the tube railways, was buried at Harrow Weald yesterday, in the presence of a distinguished company of railway magnates. The coffin was carried by six guards of the railways with which he was particularly connected.

Earlier, in July 1901, Alice Jessie DONALDSON, aged 27, had married **Charles Egerton MOTT,** aged 30, at Stanmore, Middlesex and their reception had taken place at The Moor, Stanmore, a wedding present from George DONALDSON (who was knighted in 1904) to his daughter Alice Jessie and still in the course of being built. The house was not ready for the young couple for another six months. George also provided the furniture for the house.

Charles had met Alice Jessie DONALDSON in 1898, in Stanmore, Middlesex, probably at a social function. Alice, always known as just Jessie, was small, dark haired and very shy. She was already engaged to be married to a young solicitor, Howard SWAN, but Charles nevertheless declared his love for her, but was turned down. Jessie later said she was not then in love with either suitor, but after two years she opted for Charles.

However, in 1910, their life was shattered when Sir George visited his daughter at The Moor house. The doors were opened for him by Nanny Susan PICKERING, instead of the parlour maid, and as the marble floors had just been washed she asked him, politely but firmly, to first wipe his boots on the doormat. Sir George was, to say the least, upset, and stormed in to see his daughter, without wiping his boots, and demanded that the impertinent woman should be dismissed immediately.

Lady Alice DONALDSON (standing) with Alice Jessie MOTT holding young Eric Alston MOTT, with his father, Charles Egerton MOTT c.1903. (Courtesy of the MOTT family.)

Jessie, however, stood her ground, said an apology would be insisted on but said that Nanny was excellent with the children and devoted to them. When Charles returned from a tiring day in the City he also would not hear of Susan being sacked. Sir George had left the house in a fury and as he had built the house and given it, complete with furniture, he was deeply aggrieved. The rift lasted for two years with no contact at all, but eventually Sir George resumed contact and matters healed.

Although the 1911 census showed Charles Egerton MOTT, aged 40, Solicitor, his wife Alice Jessie, aged 36, with their son Eric Alston, aged 8, and daughter Barbara Constance, aged 6, living at The Moor House, Stanmore, together with their children's nurse, Susan PICKERING, aged 52, born Bedfordshire, they were not shown as owners. (A resident cook, parlour maid and two housemaids were also present.)

No doubt because of the rift with Sir George, Charles MOTT was shown as 'Visiting Son-in-Law' and Alice Jessie, the children and nurse also all shown as visitors. It therefore appears that the MOTT family no longer regarded themselves as owners! It could also be the case that although Sir George 'gave' the house to his daughter and son-in-law, he nevertheless retained the title to it.

Charles Egerton MOTT, born Birkenhead in February 1871 and one of the two sons of Charles Grey and Sophia MOTT, is recorded as an undergraduate at Oriel College, University of Oxford, 20 October 1888, aged 17, having matriculated from Uppingham School. He rowed in the College Eight and obtained his BA in History with Honours in 1892.

After Oxford, he became an Articled Clerk to his brother-in-law, James ALSOP, a prominent Liverpool solicitor. When qualified he joined Donald McMILLAN, who had a practice at 11/12 Clements Lane in the City of London. He was able to bring valuable clients to the firm from his father, Charles Grey MOTT's, connections with the City and South London Railway Company and other railway companies.

The 1901 census records him as still living with his parents in Harrow Weald Lodge, Hendon, aged 30 and a Solicitor.

Charles and Jessie had two sons, Eric Alston, born 7 October 1902, Peter Grey, born 29 June 1913 and a daughter, Barbara Constance born in 1904, all registered in Middlesex.

In August 1914, at 44 years of age, married with three children and a growing solicitor's practice, Charles nevertheless was determined to enlist. (Conscription for single men did not start until March 1916 and for married men not until May 1916.) When he attempted to do so he was told that he was too old, but with the help of a friend at the War Office he was able to enlist in February 1915 and obtain a commission. He was gazetted 26 May 1915 as temporary Lieutenant in the Army Service Corps (later R.A.S.C.) and later recorded as Captain.

Charles Egerton MOTT c.1916. (Courtesy of the MOTT family.)

117

He served in No. 1 Company, the 53rd Welsh Division of the A.S.C. and his 'Theatre of War' was the Balkans, the peninsula that contained, among other countries, Serbia and Romania.

By October 1915, after training in military administration and logistics, he was on a troop ship bound for Suvla Bay, Gallipoli, in the British Mediterranean Expeditionary Force. He was not directly involved in the notorious military disaster, also known as the Dardanelles Campaign, in what is today modern Turkey, that took place between 25 April 1915 and 9 January 1916. Britain and France had launched a naval attack followed by an amphibious landing on the peninsula, with the aim of capturing the Ottoman capital of Constantinople (modern Istanbul).

Charles spent some three months at Suvla, in the trenches and dugouts sheltered by the cliffs or cliff tops. In the Gallipoli Campaign over 135,000 men were killed, including 68,000 Ottoman, around 56,000 British and French, 8,700 Australians and 2,700 New Zealander soldiers. Allied troops were withdrawn to Lemnos and then to Egypt, from where Charles wrote a number of letters to his son Eric.

1916

He was based in Boni Salama Camp, Warden, Egypt from where he wrote on 31 January about the dangers he experienced at Suvla. He was responsible for the receipt and issue of supplies, with a gang of 20 Egyptian labourers to fetch and carry and with many mules to care for. They were under constant shell fire, in one instance shrapnel pierced a milk case on which Charles had his hand.

The official military record of his medal entitlement, giving his address as Pendell House, Bletchingley, Surrey, showed he had the 1914–15 Star, the British War Medal and the Allied Victory Medal (pictured).

A handwritten note on the form has the rather cryptic statement 'V.M.

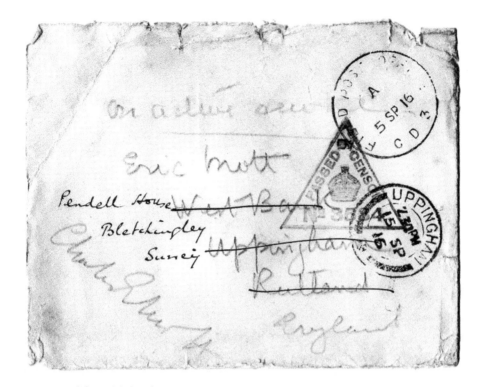

(Courtesy of the MOTT family.)

found by Police 16-8-71', so it must be assumed that the family lost the Allied Victory Medal at this time.

This letter was sent by Charles Egerton MOTT from Egypt in September 1916 to his son Eric, at his boarding school in Uppingham, Rutland but readdressed to Pendell House. It is marked 'On active service' with a stamp 'Field Post Office 5 SP 16'. Also a triangular stamp embossed 'Passed Censor No. 3584' and a post office stamp dated 15 SP 16.

Sir George Hunter DONALDSON, (1845–1925) a notable antique and fine art collector, spotted that Pendell House was for sale in 1916 whilst reading the *Country Life* magazine and decided to purchase it for his daughter, **Alice Jessie MOTT**, then aged 42. He had clearly settled the family rift and settled funds on her to allow her to maintain it.

1917

Because of the extreme anti-German feeling in the country, George V decided to change the family name from Saxe-Coburg-Gotha to the House of Windsor.

1918

The Armistice was signed at 11 a.m. on 11 November 1918 between the Allies and Germany.

Charles returned to England on leave in the spring of 1918, probably seeing his family home at Pendell House for the first time. He had spent three years in Gallipoli, Egypt and Palestine and the contrast with Blechingley must have been incredible. He had to first return to Beirut before being demobilised in 1920 and returning to his partnership in the City with Donald McMILLAN. The Westminster Bank, the firm's most important client, was expanding fast, and with it the firm of Mott & McMillan, who moved to new offices at Stafford House, 14 King William Street.

In 1923, Charles Egerton MOTT purchased a 1923 11.9hp Morris Oxford open tourer car. None of the family knew how to drive so it was delivered by a former racing driver who stayed as a guest for ten days as an instructor. A course was pegged out in the grounds and when training finished it was decided to take the family to Cornwall in the car, the 250 miles driven by Eric. A chauffeur was later employed, George BROWN, always known as 'Brownsky'. He was a short and solemn man with a military waxed moustache and, with his wife Florence, lived in the cottage at the far end of their meadow.

Charles' eldest son, Eric Alston MOTT (1902–1990), after eight years in boarding schools, went to Oriel College, Oxford University at 18. He obtained an Honours Degree in Modern History and, as a special subject, banking, currency and finance. He was a member of the Union, the University Boxing Club and the Officer Training Corps, Cavalry Squadron.

In 1924, Eric became his father's Articled Clerk, and in April 1927 passed the final examination of the Law Society and became Assistant Solicitor at a salary of £200 p.a. In November 1927, he sailed from Liverpool and spent a year travelling to Egypt, Sudan, Uganda, Kenya, India, Mandalay, Java, Hong Kong, Japan and the United States, returning to the UK in August 1928.

He married Margaret BERGER in the USA in 1929 and returned to England, settling in the outskirts of Hampstead Heath. During World War Two he had a short spell in military intelligence before being released to take charge of his practice in the City. In 1940, after Dunkirk, his wife Margaret, with their three young sons, sailed for America, living with her mother in Denver. She returned in 1943, at great personal risk, and found work with the United States Office of

War Information. Eric and Margaret divorced in 1963 and he retired in 1968 as partner from his firm, but continuing as Chairman of the Optrex organisation and Director of other companies, and died in 1990 in Langport, Somerset, at the age of 87.

In his book *Portrait of a Family* he recollects his time at Pendell House. 'Wood and coal fires in large open grates heated the living rooms and the main bedrooms to a degree or two above zero during the winter.' He recalled the three large bathrooms, built one on top of the other early in the 20th century, at the rear of the house, with domestic hot water provided by a huge boiler. He added that the house was lit by 60 oil lamps and it was his task, during school holidays, to trim 30 lamps a day.

When his grandfather, Sir George DONALDSON, died in 1925 more fine furniture and paintings were left to his parents and electricity and central heating was installed. Charles and Jessie also advertised for a gardener and within days over 40 applications were received.

After a short list and many interviews, James KETTLE, a Blechingley-born man and youngest of 23 children, was chosen and he and his wife and three children, Rosie, Betty and Alfie, moved into the first cottage adjoining the house. James KETTLE loved gardening and worked from 7 a.m. until late at night, weekends included. He had assistance at times but mostly was on his own. In addition to turning the two acres of garden and walls into outstanding flowers, fruit and vegetables, he tended his own garden, where he specialised in dahlias, cross breeding all manner of varieties.

Eric recalls that his father was an early member of the Worshipful Company of Solicitors in the City of London and had he lived would have served as Master, something that Eric attained in 1953/54. Eric says his father was, so he said, a Unitarian, 'but was ready to worship God with his fellow man, be they Catholic, Protestant, Muslim, Buddhist or Hindu'.

The entire family walked to St Mary the Virgin Church, Blechingley, every Sunday morning, taking the footpath across Thomasland via Brewer Street, past the fine old Regency Rectory and up beside the unsightly pile of buildings that had been the Poor House or Union Workhouse.

Eric states:

This grim institution then housed some 100 or more young men, locally called 'the loonies', who suffered from all manner of mental and/or emotional handicaps. They were herded along the lanes like cattle by the male staff of the Institution. They were a saddening sight. Every Sunday these dumb-oxen lads were led into the pews of the church that were specially reserved for them. The church was usually full and after the service something akin to a garden party took place in the churchyard. Everybody stopped to chat and gossip, Blechingley was a lively and tightly-knit community.

The British Legion marched on Armistice Day and placed wreaths at the Memorial Cross. Charles, with his three medals, was among the marchers. He was also on the Parish Council and when I reached the age of 21 I joined him.

Jessie was a successful President of the Women's Institute and a leader in many local activities. My brother Peter, aged 16, gave lectures on Japan in the village hall and he and my sister Barbara were leading members of the village dramatic society.

Charles and Jessie's only daughter, Barbara Constance MOTT, born 1904, went to the famous Roedean School and a domestic science establishment in Switzerland, as well as having a first-class Governess, to receive a good education, but, in Eric's words, 'all proved to have a similar effect – that of water on a duck's back'.

However, he goes on to say that 'she is highly intelligent, full of natural wisdom, endowed with a great sense of fun and humour, and has a nature that is generous to a degree. Every family needs an "Auntie Bar" and my own family is fortunate enough to have the best and most original of this species.'

Barbara married Ronald McPHERSON in 1942, who had won the Military Medal as a sergeant in the Highland Light Infantry in World War One. He died in 1961 and Barbara moved to North Cornwall.

This photo, wrongly stated as 'the MOTT boys', was given to Derek MOORE by Bill and Mollie KETTLE in 1996. Bill was the son of the Pendell House gardener and cook during the tenure of the Mott family.

Peter Grey MOTT (1913–1995) is on the right, believed to be with Erich ETIENNE, a German surveyor and Rhodes scholar who was a great friend of Peter and accompanied him on three expeditions to Greenland. Sadly, Erich was killed in World War Two.

Peter was educated at Sherborne School and, like his father and brother, went to Oriel College, Oxford, where he obtained an Honours degree in Engineering Science. Whilst at Oxford he had joined the University Exploration Society and taken part in an expedition to West Greenland. This gave him a lasting interest in surveying and exploring and he took part in further expeditions in Greenland and Switzerland. In May1939, he was awarded the Murchisan Grant of the Royal Geographical Society for this work. He was deeply involved in the use of aerial and ground photography for measurements.

(Courtesy of Derek MOORE.)

As well as the expeditions Peter led as an undergraduate to Greenland and his involvement with Eric Shipton in surveying the approaches to Mt. Everest in the Karakoram Himalaya, his pioneering contributions to aerial survey and photogrammetry should also be recorded.

In 1955, he organised the aerial survey of the Antarctic Peninsula and subsequently led the expedition over two seasons in 1956 and 1957. This involved the co-ordination of a supply ship, two Canso amphibious aircraft, a helicopter and some 20 scientists/surveyors working on the ground. 35,000 square miles of this hazardous and hitherto unmapped, but scenically mountainous and spectacular territory, was surveyed. (Peter wrote a full account, *Wings over Ice*, which was published in 1986.)

Shortly after, he left for India as chief surveyor on Eric Shipton's expedition to the Karakoram Himalaya, where in three months they mapped an area of 1,600 square miles containing the two longest glaciers outside polar regions and six peaks over 24,000ft.

The war stopped further work and Peter was commissioned in the Royal Engineers, attached to the Indian Survey Office. He served five years on the Afghan frontier and the General Staff in Delhi, with the rank of Major, finally producing maps for the Burma campaign.

Peter married Eleanor BLICKLEY, a Canadian, in Dehra Dun, India in 1940, and in 1945 the family, with his two sons, were repatriated to England, arriving in Glasgow on VE Day. His career included a Divisional Officer with the Ordnance Survey, Chief Surveyor for Hunting Aerosurvey Ltd for 32 years, with shipping, aircraft and oil interests. He played a major part in pioneering and perfecting many new ideas and techniques, including the 1970s development of the first European system for automated digital mapping.

He was elected a Fellow of the Royal Institution of Chartered Surveyors in 1951, and in 1959 was awarded the President's medal of the Photogrammetric Society and became President 1966/67. He was the Managing Director of Hunting Surveys in 1972. Eleanor died in 1967 and he later married Suzette Naomi Osborne BELL. Peter died in 1995 in Yeovil, Somerset, at the age of 82.

1921

William BELL died and the Pendell Court estate was inherited by his son, 'Archie'. The land, which included three farms and many houses, was gradually sold to mainly sitting tenants in the 1930s.

1923

The 7 September *Surrey Mirror & County Post* reported a case of theft from Pendell House.

The circumstances were that 'a pretty girl in nurse's uniform', Marguerite JENNER, otherwise known as Jenny, aged 22, appeared before the Reigate Bench charged with fraudulently obtaining board and lodgings from the South Eastern Hotel, Redhill.

However, the Head Constable told the bench that he would withdraw the charge and proceed with another charge. He alleged that between 1 May and 13 August the prisoner stole a hat, cloak, two frocks, shawl, underskirt, four camisoles, a suit of pyjamas and various other items, together valued at £6, the property of her former employer, Charles Egerton MOTT, Pendell House, Blechingley.

Susan PICKERING, the Pendell House children's nurse, gave evidence of the prisoner being employed at the house as a housemaid in April and leaving 13 August. She identified the property as taken from the house and did not know they were missing until shown them by the police, who had found them in a locked case in the possession of the prisoner. Marguerite JENNER, who had falsely stated she was a probationer nurse, and cried throughout the hearing, pleaded guilty to the theft and was sentenced to a month in prison, whereupon she was removed from the dock in hysterics.

1925

Sir George DONALDSON died after a short illness and his Will provided his daughter and Charles with substantial additions to their finances.

1925–1928

The Electoral Rolls show Pendell House as occupied by Charles MOTT, Alice MOTT, and Eric MOTT, with Barbara Constance MOTT added in 1929. The *Surrey Mirror & County Post* on 20 March 1925 reported that Charles Egerton MOTT and Eric Alston MOTT were elected to the Blechingley Parish Council.

1931

Charles Egerton MOTT died 3 December at Marylebone, London, and was buried at the early Norman *c.*1090 St Mary the Virgin Church, Blechingley.

The *Surrey Mirror & County Post*, on Friday 11 December 1931, gave a very full report of the funeral of Mr Charles Egerton MOTT at Blechingley Parish Church of St Mary the Virgin. It reported that 'the grave of Mr W. G. GREENAWAY, Mr MOTT's old batman, who served him throughout the 1914–18 war, is immediately adjacent, this being arranged at the special request of the family'. The congregation remained in church at the conclusion of the service whilst only the relatives were present at the graveside.

Full details of the hymns were given, together with a long list of those who attended. It included members of the Parish Council; the British Legion; the 'Major Barclay Lodge of Oddfellows'; the outdoor and indoor staff of Pendell House; representatives of London Underground Railways; City of London Solicitors' Company; the East Surrey Liberal Association; staff of Donald McMillan and Mott and Sir Frederick KENYON representing the British School at Jerusalem. Among the long list of floral tributes were those from Sir Morgan and Lady CROFTON; Sir Basil MOTT and family; Mrs Thornley MOTT; Mr and Mrs Adrian MOTT; Old Comrades of the R.A.S.C.; The Children at Pendell House Cottage; the staff at Weavers Warwicks Wold; the General Managers the Westminster Bank; the Directors & Officers of the City and South London Railway and the Directors of the Trevose Golf Club.

Included among the mourners were Mrs C. E. MOTT (widow); Mr & Mrs E. A. MOTT (son and daughter-in-law; Miss Barbara MOTT (daughter); Mr Peter MOTT (son); Mrs ALSOP (sister); Mrs & Miss LAMBERT (sister-in-law and niece); Mrs & Mrs BUSH JAMES (brother-in-law and sister-in-law); Mr A. WALKER (nephew); Mr Edmund DONALDSON (brother-in-law); and Brigadier General A. H. COTES JAMES and Captain E. H. O'DONNELL.

1932

The Probate Record on 18 March showed that Charles Egerton MOTT of 14 King William Street, London and of Pendell House, Blechingley, Surrey, who died 3 December 1931 at 57 Manchester Street, St Marylebone, Middlesex, left effects to the value of £18,281. 6s 11d to his widow, Alice Jessie MOTT. In 1936, Mrs Alice MOTT moved to 'a pleasant thatched house, Martins, at Abinger Hammer, Surrey' (as recollected by her grandson, Malcolm Clive McPHERSON, afterwards known as Margaret McPHERSON in his/her book *Ranger Margaret*).

She died 6 December 1958 in Torquay but Alice Jessie and Charles were buried at St Mary the Virgin Church, Blechingley. In her Will she left an exceptionally fine drawing by Thomas Gainsborough to the Ashmolean Museum, Oxford. It is in black and white chalk on green-grey paper, measuring 49cm x 30.5cm, and had belonged to her father, Sir George DONALDSON.

Mrs Margaret Berger MOTT, wife of Eric Alston MOTT, who shared the inheritance of Pendell House, travelled to Denver, Colorado in 1940 with her children, where they took wartime refuge with her mother. She returned in 1943, at great personal risk. The children stayed on in America during much of the war. Michael returned home to England in 1944 and John and Anthony followed in 1946.

(WA1959.9 Thomas Gainsborough, Study of a Woman, seen from the Back. Bequeathed by Mrs Alice Jessie Mott, in memory of her husband Charles Egerton Mott, 1959. Image © Ashmolean Museum, University of Oxford.)

The subsequent career of their three children is as follows:

Michael Charles Alston MOTT, born 8 December 1930, was commissioned in the Queen's Royal Regiment during his National Service, then went to Oriel College, Oxford, like other members of his family, and then joined his father as Articled Clerk. However, he left to follow his wish to become a writer and poet, the author of four novels, eleven collections of poetry, as well as a biography. In 1964, he accepted an appointment as writer-in-residence at Kenyon College, Ohio, and his career as a teacher of English literature followed to Atlanta, Georgia, Bowling Green, Ohio and Williamsburg, Virginia.

In 1983, St Mary's College, Notre Dame University, Indiana, conferred the degree of Doctor of Letters, honoris causa, on him and for his authorised biography of Thomas Merton he was the runner-up for the Pulitzer Prize in 1984. His papers are held at Northwestern University.

John Malcolm Donaldson MOTT, born 8 December 1932, went to Uppingham School, following the tradition started by his grandfather. and from April 1951 to April 1953 carried out his National Service in the Royal Navy. He spent two months in Suez, assisting the movement of shipping during the strike of Egyptian pilots, served in the Mediterranean for 10 months and joined a minesweeper based in Malta clearing World War Two mines from the Ionian and Aegean seas.

Standing, l. to r., Eric Alston MOTT and Peter Grey MOTT
Sitting, l. to r., Margaret Berger MOTT; 'Nan' Susan PICKERING (of upsetting Sir George
DONALDSON in 1910 fame); Michael MOTT, 6yrs; Alice Jessie MOTT holding Eric Anthony MOTT;

John returned to England in September 1952, after an adventurous voyage from Malta in an old motor launch. Following a gunnery course he joined the Elbe Squadron, based in Cuxhaven, Germany, and was given command of an ex-German air/sea rescue and patrol launch. He was promoted to Sub-Lieutenant in April 1953 and led the Elbe Squadron on a Baltic cruise before demobilisation from the Royal Navy.

He later became Managing Director of a well-known English tannery and then Partner in a firm in Woburn, Massachusetts,

Eric Anthony Grey MOTT, born 27 January 1936, on his return to England from the USA in 1945 went to Charterhouse College and during his National Service was commissioned and served in the 1st King's Dragoon Guards in Germany.

He then obtained an Honours degree in history at Trinity College, Cambridge, before starting a career in publishing. He became Editor-in-Chief of Penguin Books and later formed his own publishing company, Anthony Mott Ltd.

THE STURGE FAMILY

1936

Raymond Wilson STURGE, born 10 June 1904, Bromley, Kent and his wife, **Margaret Sylvia**, née KEEP, born 16 December 1906 in Sydney, were married in September 1929 in Groombridge, and purchased Pendell House in 1936. He was the son of Arthur Lloyd and Jessie Le STURGE of Chislehurst, Kent. His father was an Underwriter who formed A. L. STURGE HOLDINGS, one of the largest underwriting agencies in the Lloyd's insurance market.

The 1911 census showed the family living in Chislehurst with Arthur, 43 years; Gwendolyn, daughter, 11 years; Rona Winifred, daughter, 10 years; Raymond Wilson, son, 6 years and Katharine Brenda, daughter, 3 years. Also in the household were a Cook, two Nurses, two Parlour Maids and a Housemaid.

Son Raymond, also originally an Underwriter at Lloyds, became Chairman of A. L. STURGE HOLDINGS from 1955 to 1969, when he retired. He also became Chairman of Lloyds from 1964 to 1965. At that time, the family had a Cook, Kitchen Maid, Housemaid, Parlour Maid, Under Parlour Maid, Children's Nanny (May KNIGHT), Maid, Chauffeur, Gardener (Mr KETTLE), Assistant Gardener (Mr DAY) and a Garden Boy.

The first room on the left on entering the front door was then known as The Library and the adjoining room (second door on left) was the Dining Room. The kitchen was in the basement and the first-floor room at the front south-west corner was the Children's Room with an adjoining Nursery in the north-west corner. This is why there is a communicating door on the west side of the two rooms.

Edward, Prince of Wales, succeeded to the throne on the death of his father, Edward VII, and became Edward VIII. However, he abdicated before being crowned, renouncing the throne so he could marry Mrs SIMPSON, an American divorcée. George VI, Edward's brother, thus became king.

Alan TURING developed the first device that printed symbols on paper tape following a series of logical instructions, forming the foundations of the computer as we know it today.

1937
Whilst Mr and Mrs STURGE were carrying out some alterations to the property, early that year, someone smelt smoke, opened the then dining room door at the south-east corner of the building and saw that the entire room was alight. The door was slammed shut to contain the oxygen, so the fire had not spread by the time the Fire Brigade arrived to successfully extinguish the fire.

1939
3 September saw the outbreak of World War Two.

Raymond STURGE joined the Royal Scots Fusiliers and ended up as Major at Aldershot responsible for planning duties, in particular those for D-Day.

The gardeners were reduced to one but there was no usual chauffeur upkeep of the extensive lawns, which became a problem. The Orchard became a hay field, as did the Tennis Court lawn, although part of that was dug up for vegetables.

1940
Pendell House was requisitioned by the Woman's Royal Army Corps (WRACS) and then by Canadian soldiers, but was handed back to the STURGE family in 1943.

1943

St Mary the Virgin Church, Blechingley, burial records for July state that three German airmen were buried, named K. DUBIAK, H. H. DUNZELT and the third unknown. They were exhumed 31 October 1962 and transported to the German War Cemetery, Cannock Chase, Stafford.

The Colossus, the first electric programmable computer, was developed in December by Tommy FLOWERS to enable British code breakers to read German Enigma code signals.

1944

1 June saw the first of the V1 flying bombs launched from France by the Germans. These were so-called because they were Vengeance weapons and fell randomly directly their fuel ran out.

Mrs Anne MITCHELL, a close family friend living at Pendell House, was on the phone *c.*1944 when she saw a V1 travelling towards her. She said to her friend, 'If I am not talking to you in 10 seconds I will probably be dead.' As it was, the bomb fell in Cockley Wood, short of the building. Portions of the bomb were later found in the wood and this photo was taken of a large piece.

(Courtesy of Derek MOORE.)

130

Charlie STURGE also recalls this incident. He says:

> *It was at 11 a.m. that day in 1944 that I and members of my family were standing in the hall when we heard the noise of the 'doodlebug' engine close by, not having had time to shelter in the basement. Just hearing the engine cut out was scary enough without witnessing the V1 approaching. My mother always liked to say Anne was sitting in the Library talking to her bank manager, looking out of the window towards Cockley Wood. She had a bird's eye view and of course knew when the engine cut out that her number was up.*

There was then a tremendous explosion, with some windows blown in but the bomb had lost height and got caught in the trees of Cockley Wood. Although it fell in the woods at the front of Pendell House, it was strange that the blast blew in the windows at the back of the house, as well as the basement kitchen window next to the road.

Charlie added that during this period the family spent the nights in the basement as they never knew when a flying bomb was going to drone over. They often hit the North Downs when they lost height.

6 June was D-Day, the invasion of Europe.

1945

End of World War Two was on 8 May, known as VE Day.

The first atom bomb was dropped on Hiroshima, Japan on 6 August, followed by one on Nagasaki on 9 August. This resulted in the surrender of Japan with VJ Day celebrated on 15 August.

The highest rate of income tax peaked in World War Two at 99.25%. It was then slightly reduced and was around 90% through the 1950s and 1960s. Because of this, a 'striving market garden' was created at Pendell House but, as stated by Charlie STURGE, 'I doubt it made much money but it made a good tax break'. (The top rate of income tax on earned income was not cut to 75% until 1971 but the basic rate has been progressively cut until the current 20%.)

The STURGE family made a number of dramatic changes to the building after the war. The basement kitchen was turned into a laundry room and a new ground floor kitchen created in the north-east corner of the house. The dining room was changed to the north-west corner of the house and the former south-east corner dining room changed to a smaller study with an adjacent pantry adjoining the kitchen. An en suite bathroom was created in what had been the Nurse's Bedroom on the first floor south-east corner of the house, with a passageway through the cupboard into the Master Bedroom in the north-east part of the house.

What had been the Children's Room on the first floor south-west corner of the house became the spare room and a bathroom made in the small room leading off it. The Nursery survived as the Nanny remained until the house was sold in 1969.

1946

The London Electoral Register showed that the STURGE family also had a town house at 37 Lime Street, Cornhill, in the City of London financial centre. This house was the office of A. L. Sturge Holdings. Lloyd's was kept open during the war, staffed by over-50s, and it is possible that those members of the staff used the office as 'their home'.

1947

Raymond STURGE obtained permission to use Prisoners of War to dig out the lily pond in the garden and create a swimming pool.

Members of the Surrey Archaeological Society visited Pendell House on 10 June 'by kind permission of Mr and Mrs Raymond Sturge'.

1950

Article in the *West Australian* newspaper on 5 February:

> *Mrs. Raymond Sturge set out from England yesterday week to fly to Sydney by way of America to attend the wedding of her niece in Sydney yesterday. She finally reached Mascot at 6.30 o'clock last night, a little more than three hours after the wedding had taken place. She found that she was even too late to congratulate the couple, Mr. and Mrs. Peter Chambers (the bride was formerly Miss Margot Keep), who left for their honeymoon at Surfers' Paradise about the time she reached the city.*

1951

On 18 July, *The Tatler* reported the marriage of Mr Peter Wyatt KININMONTH, younger son of Mr and Mrs A. M. KININMONTH of Caxton, Marlow, Bucks to Miss Priscilla Margaret STURGE, eldest daughter of Mr and Mrs Raymond STURGE of Pendell House, Bletchingley, Surrey.

1952

Queen Elizabeth II came to the throne when her father died on 6 February.

1955

The *Wiltshire Times and Trowbridge Advertiser* reported that on Saturday 5 February, Diana Catherine STURGE, the second daughter of Raymond and Margaret STURGE, married John Dawson ECCLES, elder son of Sir David ECCLES, Minister for Education, at the Church of St Mary the Virgin, Blechingley.

The Bishop of Southwark officiated, assisted by the Master of the Temple, Canon J. FIRTH. The bride was attended by her sisters, Miss Caroline and Miss Sara STURGE. Lord Nicholas GORDON LENNOX was best man. *(Lt GORDON LENNOX was the author's Company Officer when in Germany, BAOR, 1950/52, attached to the 1st Battalion the King's Royal Rifle Corps, the 60th Rifles.)*

The Groom, John ECCLES, had gained his commission in the King's Royal Rifle Corps prior to graduating at Oxford. His late father was a noted Harley Street surgeon and he was the grandson of the late Lord DAWSON of PENN, King George V's surgeon.

1957

The Tatler on 26 June reported that Mrs Raymond STURGE would be holding

a dance at Pendell House, Blechingley, for her daughter, Miss Caroline STURGE's début and her son, Mr Anthony STURGE's coming-of-age.

1958

Pendell House received its Grade 1 listing on 11 June.

The listed building plaque on the right of the front door.

1961

The Tatler on 15 February reported in its list of 'Dates for Debutantes' that: 'Mrs Raymond STURGE and Mrs Arthur SKIPWITH will be holding a reception at Pendell House, Blechingley, for Miss Sara STURGE and Miss Sara Jane and Miss Ann SKIPWITH (twins) on Friday 15 September.'

Pendell Court was purchased by The Hawthorns Pre-Prep (for pupils aged 2 to 7) and Preparatory Day School (for pupils aged 7 to 13).

The Sturge family in 1966.
Back row, left to right: Charles STURGE, Diana ECCLES (née STURGE), James RUCKER, Caroline RUCKER (née STURGE), Peter KININMONTH, Priscilla KININMONTH (née STURGE), John ECCLES.
Second row; Stephen IRWIN, Alexander KININMONTH, Mr Raymond STURGE with Rupert RUCKER in his arms, Mrs Margaret STURGE with Tiffany STURGE in her arms, Denise STURGE with Lisa STURGE in arms, Sara IRWIN (née STURGE), James KININMONTH.
Front row: Alice, William, Catherine and Emily – all ECCLES, David and Philippa KININMONTH.

1969

Raymond STURGE retired and sold Pendell House, together with 20 acres, for £30,000 having paid £6,000 in 1936. He retired to Dorset, where he died 30 March

1984, aged 80, at Lord's Mead, Ashmore. His wife Margaret died in 1995, aged 89.

It is believed that the house was sold to Eric Schemilt Designs Ltd, a renowned fashion designer, incorporated 28 April 1966.

A carrier bag they designed for an associate, Elio Fiorucci (1935–2015) is in the Victoria & Albert Museum. They traded from 33/34 Chancery Lane, London, and a publicity poster featuring Santa Claus riding on a spaceship, and another featuring the rear view of a girl wearing white boots on a beach, which they also designed for Fiorucci, are on show in the National Gallery of Australia.

Fiorucci was well known for their wearable 'pop art' on such items as scarves and it is thought that Elio also shared Pendell House with Eric Schemilt. As a leader in the globalisation of fashion, Fiorucci would scour the globe, introducing a newly affluent mass market to underground trends such as thongs from Brazil and Afghan coats.

The label popularised camouflage prints and leopard-skin prints before creating the designer jean market with the invention of stretch jeans. The iconic advertising usually featured a woman's buttocks in skin-tight denim, or in one case obscured by pink fluffy handcuffs, whilst the company logo is two cheeky angels modelled after Raphael's cherubs. However, financial problems led to receivership in 1989, and since then the brand has been dogged by legal battles over the trademarks, and several re-launches have failed to make much impact.

(Elio Fiorucci was found dead in his Milan home on 20 July 2015, at the age of 80. Relatives say he was in 'good health' before his death, but he may have succumbed to sudden illnesses later on.)

1973

On 4 October, Surrey County Council Planning Department granted Listed Building Consent to B. C. HARRIS Esq. to remove existing brick filling from original window opening on west elevation, insert stone surround and sliding sash window to match existing windows at Pendell House, 'the materials and finishes shall match those of the existing windows and surrounds'.

1982

Peter John SCOTT purchased Pendell House.

Although it was not possible to make contact with him, enquiries reveal that he is said to have once been Chairman of Aegis, a Media Buyer organisation (Aegis is ancient Greek for a shield) and in 1988 a Director of Virgin Management Ltd.

It is believed that in 1995 he founded the Test Valley Water Company and was a Director until June 2003, when the company dissolved. The water on his land was sold as 'Ashe Park' mineral water. He is also said to have been one of the lead partners in a 2004 Management Buy Out Team that ran WCRS, a London Advertising Agency. (He had originally founded the company with Robin WRIGHT and Peter SCOTT was the 'S' in the company name.)

On 9 February 2017, he was appointed Director of The Physical Network Ltd, a company that supplies software for event organisers, especially music festivals. It is said that he has held 91 directorships, of which 14 were at one time currently active.

Although none of this information can be confirmed, there is every reason to believe it is correct.

1987

David DRISCOLL purchased Pendell House with 45 acres, together with the four rear cottages. He was, and is, a Director of a family property company, now in Woodford Green, Essex, with his son, also David, and daughters Lynne DRISCOLL and Mrs Karen FROGGATT.

Lynne DRISCOLL lived in the coach house at the rear of Pendell House. Her horses were also stabled there. She started her career as a show jumper whilst living at Pendell House and went on to represent Great Britain as a member of the British showjumping team, competing on National cups for many years. She rode under her then married name of Lynne van HEYNINGEN and was the fifth ranked lady rider in the UK.

She currently owns Ringlands Stables, Grays Road, Biggin Hill. In May 2012, the then Metropolitan Commissioner, Sir Bernard Hogan-Howe, made a visit to Ringlands Stables to learn about the Safer Saddle Scheme, which had been operating there since 2008. The Commissioner, who rides in his spare time, was introduced to one of Lynne's horses, British showjumper Al Capone, who is known in the stable as Eric.

David and Barbara DRISCOLL in centre, with his mother Mrs Jessie DRISCOLL, and daughter Lynne.

David DRISCOLL with his father David, on his wedding day to Kim TIERENA in 1988.

1989

On 4 April, Tandridge District Council Planning Dept. granted Listed Building Consent to Mr & Mrs D. DRISCOLL for the formation of a landscaped bank adjacent to the M23 and an amended plan showing a lorry entrance and exit solely from Pendell Road:

> *Providing that the new planting shown on the approved drawings shall be carried out during the first planting season after commencement of the development, and that any trees or shrubs dying or being removed within 5 years after planting shall be replaced by a tree or shrub of similar size and species. No work on the formation of the landscaped bank shall take place on Saturdays, Sundays or Bank Holidays.*
>
> *The material to be deposited at the site in connection with the formation of the bank shall be as specified in the letter of 3 March 1989 and drawing DGO5 such that topsoil shall be evenly spread and deeply cultivated so as to ensure that any compacted layers are effectively broken up and that landscaping on the bank can take place.*

Whilst preparing for excavated soil for the Bund, he discovered the original sedan chair gates, in a poor condition, buried outside the walled garden and had new ones made to the same design. The Bund covered the grounds to the west and south of the site, adjacent to the M23, and also covered the stream that ran from Pendell Court, under the road, to the south of the Pendell House main entrance. A tunnel therefore had to be built, creating a small pond during the process, to ensure that the stream continued on its path to the west.

1990

On 13 March, Tandridge District Council Planning Dept. granted Listed Building Consent to Mr & Mrs D. DRISCOLL for the erection of a garage block/farm store south west of Pendell House and access improvements with a 2m high boundary wall/fence, to ensure that the new works harmonise with the existing building.

THE HESKETH FAMILY

John HESKETH, MA (Oxon), M.Econ, BSc. purchased Pendell House in 1990. After Oxford and London Universities he went to the United Nations on a Geneva interne programme, then to Australia where, after five years doing a Masters Degree by thesis, was appointed as the first 'Australian' to the OECD in Paris. He was granted dual nationality and Australian citizenship by the Australian Prime

Minister so that he could read Austeo communications.

John then set up Forex Research in London and New York, forecasting exchange rates. At the same time (1990) he switched to property conservation and development, purchasing Barham Court in Kent and Pendell House in Surrey. Barham Court was designed by the US 'Father of American Architecture' Benjamin Henry LATROBE in the 1790s.

John HESKETH.

1991

On 19 March, Tandridge District Council Planning Dept. refused Listed Building Consent to Mr & Mrs B. C. J. HESKETH for a variation of the bund size and boundaries as approved under 88/1324.

The reasons for the refusal were:

The steepness of the slopes of the bund on the western side are unsatisfactory and likely to lead to long term instability to the detriment of the adjacent M23 Motorway embankment.

In view of the possibility of the widening of the M23 Motorway the Council is not satisfied that the compaction of the material used in the construction of the bund will not be prejudicial to the Secretary of State's proposals.

The proposed work does not provide for the provision of drainage to prevent silting up of the adjacent motorway drainage ditch and motorway culvert nor the run-off of material at the northern end onto Pendell Road.

The proposal does not provide for the satisfactory routing and re-routing of Footpath 172 Bletchingley – Pendell House.

On 13 September, Mr B. C. J. HESKETH applied to convert the stables and garden store into two cottages, together with alterations to the existing two cottages and the erection of four car ports and four parking spaces. This was approved 28 January 1992.

Some of the main restorative work carried out during his occupation was to the basement floor.

THE MILNER-BROWN FAMILY

1997

Pendell House was purchased by David and Amanda MILNER-BROWN on 3 June. They met at university and married in 1980. David's parents, Martin and Elizabeth MILNER, were of Manchester origin, where Martin was the renowned Leader of the internationally known Hallé Orchestra. On leaving university, David became a manager for the business consultancy organisation Arthur Anderson, and was later Partner for a similar organisation, Accenture.

Amanda, once her sons were adults, took up writing and in 2005 wrote *Foul Deeds & Suspicious Deaths in Guildford,* followed by *Foul Deeds & Suspicious Deaths in Croydon,* under the pen-name of Caroline Maxton.

140

David and Amanda MILNER-BROWN at their wedding in 1980.

One of the first improvements to the house, specified in June 1997, was a sophisticated combined fire and burglar alarm system, covering all entries and floors, fitted by SSAIB Security Systems & Alarms Inspection Board. It had a 10-minute delay on activation, at police request, but also had an unusual feature.

A wartime Air Raid Warning Siren was found to be still fitted on the roof, giving warning to the whole of Blechingley! The new alarm system was therefore fitted to this rooftop siren, in addition to the internal 110 Db sounders.

The siren had been set for the 'All Clear' continuous high-pitched sound, rather than the 'Up and Down' warbling sound indicating the approach of enemy aircraft. This continuous sound was discovered by one of their sons when he accidently set off the alarm!

Tandridge District Council Planning Dept. gave planning permission on 6 June for the installation of a private sewage treatment plant and repairs to the existing drains.

On 14 November, Listed Building Consent was given for restoration works to garden and forecourt walls, including re-pointing, replacement of missing ball finials and replacement of modern iron gates with wooden gates.

There were conditions that (a) the mortar used shall be a 3:1 mix of graded sand to lime putty and prior to the work commencing a sample panel shall be prepared and submitted for approval; (b) to ensure that the new works harmonise with the existing building to ensure a good match and protect the character of the listed wall.

1998

Permission was given 26 January to fell 55 conifer trees and reduce approx. 100 conifers by 6 metres. 'Footpath 172 Rights of Way not to be obstructed.'

1999

On 15 June, Tandridge District Council Planning Dept. granted permission to Mr P. A. ROWLAND, Evergreen Tree Services, to fell a weeping ash, thin two cherry trees by 20–30 per cent and remove secondary stem of a eucalyptus tree at Pendell House, on condition he had the permission of the owners of the trees in question.

An earlier application, 9 April 1998. had the proviso that footpath No.172, in close proximity to the proposed works, should not at any time be obstructed by associated debris, such as piles of brushwood, fallen trees or mounds of burning material.

2000

On 26 April, Tandridge District Council Planning Dept. granted permission for the erection of new access gates together with the realignment of the driveway.

On 22 August, they granted Listed Building Consent to Mr & Mrs D. MILNER-BROWN for internal alterations to the dining room and bedrooms. This involved removing the north wall of the dining room, restoring it to its original size, moving the access door from near the entrance to its original position and exposing the fireplace, which had been hidden. This meant that the walk-in pantry of the kitchen was removed but the dining room could now accommodate more people.

On 27 September, Tandridge District Council Planning Dept. granted Listed Building Consent to Mr and Mrs D. MILNER-BROWN for the renovation/ replacement of internal plumbing, electrical and heating services. This was necessary for the changing of a first floor bedroom into a large en-suite for the main bedroom. This was later called the 'Emperor Suite'.

During the early part of the 21st century the tunnel, built in 1989 by David DRISCOLL to carry the stream under the Bund, collapsed. This created a serious problem as it assisted to drain any overflow from the large pond in adjacent Pendell Court. The tunnel and brickwork at its start had to be rebuilt, at considerable expense, partly paid for by insurance. At the same time, the small pond was drained to clear the silt that had accumulated.

THE HESKETH FAMILY

2005
John HESKETH re-purchased Pendell House on 6 June. After living in Pendell House for two years with his wife and family, he rented it out and some of the tenants sub-let the house to various organisations. (This included some filming for 'Playboy' videos, with John's permission.)

The organisations that were sub-let included:

2011
May – Self-catering holiday accommodation plus weddings and special events
   Incorporated 6 July 2011 – Hurstpierpoint Park Ltd, buying & selling real
   estate, later dissolved.

2012
   Incorporated 26 February– Premier Events (London) Ltd, later dissolved.
   Incorporated 26 June – Riverside Café Bar Ltd, later dissolved.
   Incorporated 19 September – Pendell House Hospitality Ltd, dissolved
   10 June 2014.

2013
On 1 May, Tandridge District Council Planning Dept. refused Listed Building Consent to Mr B. C. John HESKETH's application on 25 February to remove a section of wall and install a fire door and display of illuminated fire exit signage.

The reason for the construction was to enable a fully protected escape route from the bedrooms on the second floor of the c.1905 rear extension, together with 'always on' lighting in the hallways to better illuminate the fire escape routes. The application had been made to regularise existing works carried out to allow possible wedding/letting use.

Their reason for refusal was 'the formation of a doorway in the position in which it is located, together with its inappropriate manner in which it has been

The offending door (since removed and wall reinstated).

formed and its detailing, has resulted in significant harm to the special interest of the Grade I listed building, contrary to Saved Local Plan Policy HEI and advice contained within the NPPF'.

2014

John HESKETH sold Pendell House to the current occupier, a private individual who lives there with his family. (He allowed the author to visit and take photos of the chimney, as well as taking and forwarding the photo of the basement well.)

John is currently a Visiting Professor of Economics, mainly to the United States on International Trade, a developer of property, mainly in the UK, Bahamas and Spain and also a Conservative Councillor for Tewkesbury Borough Council.

He is currently planning to develop Pendell Parklands into a small hamlet with park (with statue of Inigo Jones) and lake.

6. APPENDIX A

NOTICES IN ST MARY THE VIRGIN CHURCH, BLECHINGLEY

The tower is early Norman (*c.* 1090) and over 5ft thick in parts. At one time there was a spire, but in 1606 this was destroyed by lightning which 'did in very short time cause the spire to burn ... and melt to infinite fragments a goodly ring of bells'. Fortunately, the bells were restored and over the centuries the numbers increased to their present ring of ten, the last two being installed in 1991.

The Curate from 1965 to 1967 was a South African studying at Kings College, London, who went on to become the well-known Archbishop Desmond TUTU.

Because of the quality of the lighting in the church, plus the reflection from either brass plate or glass when using flash or a torch, it was not possible to satisfactorily photograph most of the actual images. However, it was possible to read them, plus the East Surrey Family History Society have copied many of them as Monumental Inscriptions 1859–1942.

St Mary The Virgin Church, Blechingley.

They are therefore all reproduced as follows:

The Glory be to God alone

To the Memory of A Good man prudent As well as pious

One that in his time was very useful being always ready

To do his good Offices to all Sorts of People

RICHARD GLYD Esq. deceased

Sometimes of Pendhill in this Parrish of Bletchingley, & once

A worthy Treasurer of Christs Hospital London during 11 years who with

ELIZ (EVANS)

his wife Lyes Buryed here nigh.

By her he had several children vizr.

RICHARD, JOHN, ABRAHAM, CHARLES, ELIZth, ANN & MARY,

JOHN, CHARLES, ABRAHAM, & MARY Dyed young unmarried

ELIZ

Dyed & left no Child but was married first to

Mr. WILLm BEWLY & then to **Mr. RICH. CHANDLER**

ANN Was married to **Mr. WILLm. WRIGHT**

and has had many Children

RICHARD & his sister **ELIZth**

were rare and Excellent Christians and also Gifted with very Choice & great

Endowmts of Mind, Insomuch as to have been Kin to them is to have been Kin

to Greatness and Nobility indeed that is to Vertue & Goodness

This **RICHARD GLYD** the son (who lyes Buryed here nigh) by

ANN (STOUGHTON) His Wife had eight Children vizt.

JOHN, RICHd. & LAWRENCE

MARTHA TWO ELIZths & two ANNS

JOHN lived to be A Barrester of Grays Inn

of Some years Standing & in Practice being

a Lawyer of Sound Judgmt. Good Learning & very fair Reputation as well for

His Morals as for his Religion And being one of

The Parliament Men for this Burough of Bletchingley

So dyed (unmarried) AD MDCLXXXIX *(1689)* & Lyes Buried here nigh
LAWRENCE, RICHd & one of ye **ELIZths** & one of ye **ANNs** dyed children.
MARTHA was married to **Mr. RALPH DRAKE**
& both He and She lye Buryed here nigh having Left Six Children
ye Other **ELIZth** lived till about 18 & then dyed unmarried & lyes Buryed here nigh
the other **ANN** is married to **WILLm BROCKMAN**
of Beachburrough in Kent Esqr. & has children
Recollected AD MDCC *(1700)* by (M.G.)
One of ye oblidged Nephews of the above. Treasurer.

Here lyeth the body of **JOHN GLYD**
late of Pendhill in this Parish, Esquire,
Barrister at Law, of the Society of Gray's Inn,
one of the Burgesses for the Borough of Blechingley
in the first Parliament of their Majesties King William and Queen Mary
who departed this life the 23rd day of November 1689

Sacred to the Memory of
WILLIAM PELLATT
who departed this life 11 June 1801 aged 73 years.

To the memory of
Dame MARY BENSLEY widow of
Sir WILLIAM BENSLEY
and for twelve years his devoted wife
She was a humble. Charitable and pious Christian

In Memory of
Sir WILLIAM BENSLEY Bart
who in the early Part of his Life was an active and meritorious
Officer in His Majesty's Navy and was afterwards employed
In various Situations of Trust and Importance in Bengal in the service
of the Honourable East India Company. The eminent Ability & inflexible
Integrity which he had invariably displayed on every occasion
procured him in the Year 1781 a Seat in the East India Direction
the Duties of which Situation he continue to discharge with unabated

Zeal and Fidelity, till the Age of 73 when on the 17th day of December 1809
he died in the Hope of a more blessed and exalted Existence/

He married 12th June 1798
MARY (Sister of **JOSEPH SEYMOUR BISCOE** Esq)
of this Parish and daughter of
VINCENT JOHN BISCOE Esq
by Lady **MARY SEYMOUR**, only daughter of **EDWARD**
(8th Duke of Somerset) who died 29th Feb. 1830 aged 71
Also of **Mr JOHN PERKINS** who died November 20th 1777 aged 70 years
and **Mrs. MARGARET PERKINS** his wife
who died March 23rd 1798 aged 82 years

Sacred to the memory of
Mrs MARGARET PERKINS
sister of the late **JOHN PERKINS** Esqre.
of Pendhill Court in this parish who died July 27th 1827
Also to the memory of
MARGARET daughter of the above named
JOHN PERKINS Esqre who died 10th of May 1833

In Memory of **MARIA TROTTER**
Who died December XXVII MDCCCLXI (27th 1861)

In the vault beneath rest the mortal remains of
The Revd **JARVIS KENRICK**
Fifty years vicar of Chilham, Kent died the 7th of May 1809 aged 72
and of
DOROTHY, His wife, daughter of **WILLIAM SEWARD** Esq.
died the 8th September 1803 aged 61

Also of **WILLIAM**
Eldest son of the above
Seventeen years one of His Majesty's Justices of Great Sessions for North Wales
died at Broome In the Parish of Betchworth in this county
The 22nd of October 1829 aged 55 Leaving issue one son and three daughters

FRANCES ANNE Widow of the above named

WILLIAM KENRICK

Died Febry 8th 1811 aged 77 & was buried at Rusthall, Kent

The above plaque reads:

Sacred to the memory of

The Revd **JARVIS KENRICK**

35 years rector of this Parish who died the 21st of November 1838

in the 64th year of his age and of

MARY widow of the above

who died 31 May 1859 aged 81 years

Also to **FRANCES**

youngest daughter of **JARVIS** and **MARY KENRICK**

who died the 24th of August 1834 in the 20th year of her age.

In memory of

CLARA KENRICK

who died April 7 A.D. 1880

In memory of

JARVIS KENRICK 1852–1949

& his wife

LILIAN HELEN

1861–1925

sometime of Pendell House

This tablet is erected by their nine daughters.

THE KENRICK FAMILY

JOHN KENRICK of Welsh origin, lived at Flore in Godstone and married in 1681 Sarah TROTT, sister of Martha, wife of Sir Robert CLAYTON of Marden. Their 6th son was Matthew KENRICK (of the Middle Temple).

Matthew's 2nd son was John, 1735–1799, MP for Blechingley and Lord of the Manor.

His 3rd son was Matthew, 1730–1803, Rector of Blechingley and Lord of the Manor (a 'Squarson'), the youngest was Jarvis, Vicar of Chilham (here recorded).

JARVIS KENRICK's 2nd son, also Jarvis, succeeded his uncle as Rector of Blechingley (here recorded) and his wife, Mary, daughter of John PERKINS of Pendell Court in this parish, built the North Aisle in 1856.

Their son Jarvis, 1805–1879, was Rector of Caterham and his son Jarvis, 1852–1949, was the last KENRICK to live in Blechingley.

The Kenrick Family – 1851–1916.

The Mott Family – 1916–1936.

The Sturge Family – 1936–1969.

ND - #0325 - 270225 - C0 - 234/156/10 - PB - 9781780915524 - Gloss Lamination